D0021742

Mythmaker

The Life of J.R.R. Tolkien, Creator of *The Hobbit* and *The Lord of the Rings*

Anne E. Neimark

WITHDRAWN

HARCOURT CHILDREN'S BOOKS
Houghton Mifflin Harcourt
Boston New York

COPYRIGHT © 1996, 2012 BY ANNE NEIMARK

ALL RIGHTS RESERVED. FOR INFORMATION ABOUT PERMISSION TO
REPRODUCE SELECTIONS FROM THIS BOOK, PLEASE WRITE TO PERMISSIONS,
HOUGHTON MIFFLIN HARCOURT PUBLISHING COMPANY,
215 PARK AVENUE SOUTH, NEW YORK, NEW YORK 10003.

HARCOURT CHILDREN'S BOOKS IS AN IMPRINT OF
HOUGHTON MIFFLIN HARCOURT PUBLISHING COMPANY.

WWW.HMHBOOKS.COM

POEM, PP. 39–40, FROM *THE BOOK OF LOST TALES, PART II*, J.R.R. TOLKIEN.
COPYRIGHT © 1984 BY FRANK RICHARD WILLIAMSON AND CHRISTOPHER
REUEL TOLKIEN AS EXECUTORS OF THE ESTATE OF J.R.R. TOLKIEN. REPRINTED BY
PERMISSION OF HOUGHTON MIFFLIN HARCOURT. ALL RIGHTS RESERVED.

SONG AND RIDDLE, P. 64, FROM *THE HOBBIT* BY J.R.R. TOLKIEN.
COPYRIGHT © 1966 BY J.R.R. TOLKIEN. REPRINTED BY PERMISSION OF
HOUGHTON MIFFLIN HARCOURT. ALL RIGHTS RESERVED.

POEM, P. 71, FROM *THE TWO TOWERS*. COPYRIGHT © 1965 BY J.R.R. TOLKIEN.
COPYRIGHT © RENEWED 1993 BY CHRISTOPHER R. TOLKIEN, JOHN F. R. TOLKIEN,
AND PRISCILLA M. A. R. TOLKIEN. REPRINTED BY PERMISSION OF HOUGHTON
MIFFLIN HARCOURT. ALL RIGHTS RESERVED.

THE LIBRARY OF CONGRESS HAS CATALOGED THE ORIGINAL HARDCOVER EDITION AS
FOLLOWS:
NEIMARK, ANNE E.
MYTHMAKER: J.R.R. TOLKIEN/ANNE E. NEIMARK: ILLUSTRATED BY BRAD WEINMAN.
P. CM.
SUMMARY: FOLLOWS THE LIFE AND WORK OF THE RENOWNED FANTASY WRITER,
CREATOR OF HOBBITS, MIDDLE-EARTH, AND *THE LORD OF THE RINGS*.
1. TOLKIEN, J.R.R. (JOHN RONALD REUEL), 1892–1973 — BIOGRAPHY —
JUVENILE LITERATURE. 2. AUTHORS, ENGLISH — 20TH CENTURY — BIOGRAPHY —
JUVENILE LITERATURE. 3. FANTASTIC LITERATURE — AUTHORSHIP — JUVENILE
LITERATURE. 4. MIDDLE-EARTH (IMAGINARY PLACE) — JUVENILE LITERATURE. [1.
TOLKIEN, J.R.R. (JOHN RONALD REUEL), 1892–1973. 2. AUTHORS, ENGLISH.]
I. WEINMAN, BRAD, ILL. II. TITLE.
PR6039.032Z697 1996
828'.91209 — DC20 96-4196
ISBN 978-0-15-298847-0
ISBN 978-0-547-99734-6 (UPDATED HARDCOVER EDITION)

THE TEXT WAS SET IN JENSON.

MANUFACTURED IN THE UNITED STATES OF AMERICA
DOC 10 9 8 7 6 5 4 3 2 1
4500374666

To Alyssa Ashley Neimark—
May all your life be filled with magic and wonder

Introduction

GENERATION AFTER GENERATION OF READERS discovers J.R.R. Tolkien. His amazing mythology — grand and unique in scope — fills his popular, award-winning fantasy books: *The Hobbit*, *The Lord of the Rings*, and *The Silmarillion*. Tolkien's world of Middle-earth seems, in many ways, familiar to us. But just when we feel most comfortable with it, we're shocked, terrified, or awed by his abundance of remarkable creatures — elves, trolls, goblins, giants, dragons, Ents, Balrogs, and Orcs.

In 1936, when the ten-year-old son of an English publisher urged his father to publish *The Hobbit*, J.R.R. Tolkien's fantasy writing began its journey toward bestseller lists in dozens of countries. *The Lord of the Rings*, translated into more than thirty-five languages, is one of the most popular works of fiction in publishing history. It has sold many millions of copies, prompting radio,

TV, and movie adaptations; video games; a musical; a symphony; calendars; artwork; postcards; and dolls.

Tolkien's heroes are often "ordinary folk," bravely fighting the timeless battle between Good and Evil. "I've always been impressed," Tolkien once said, "that we are here, surviving, because of the indomitable courage of quite small people against impossible odds."

Born in 1892 in Bloemfontein, South Africa, Tolkien endured a tragic and poverty-stricken childhood. He was educated through scholarships and the support of a kind but stern priest, and graduated from England's Oxford University with impressive achievement in philology, the study of language. Later, as an Oxford professor, Tolkien won academic fame by publishing renowned works and inventing his own languages. He was, however, far more than a scholar. Within him burned an imagination so startling and unparalleled that it burst forth into his unforgettable tales of moral courage, danger, and beauty (often causing colleagues to discredit him). Tolkien's life, spent mostly in England, brought him both darkness and joy; his response was to create the magic and mythology of Middle-earth, founded on his love of language and using his knowledge of Old Norse, Germanic, and Icelandic myths. Most of his poems and stories show a reverence for the past and for uncorrupted land. And even though his villains may not be totally vanquished, it is Tolkien's heroes who endure.

J.R.R. Tolkien took fantasy, myth, and fairy tales very seriously, finding them as important for adults as for children. "Fantasy," he wrote, "remains a human right." This biography shows us the fascinating and inspiring man behind his mythology.

Chapter 1

THE TALL GRASS OF THE desert farm in Bloemfontein, Africa, almost hid him from view. His nurse screamed his name, her voice chasing him, but he kept running from her — a pale three-year-old child in a white blouse and shorts.

He loved the prickle of wild grass against his face and the bright clusters of flowers. Stopping to bend down, he yanked off his shoes and socks. "Ronald!" his nurse shouted, but she was still far behind him, her dark face wet from the sun.

He ran with bare feet pummeling the dry earth, stalks of grass bending and cracking near their roots. Now he could see the camelthorn tree on the hill! Once, his father had taken him to this nearby farm, lifting him onto a limb of the tree. He'd wrapped his legs around the warm, scratchy bark. "We don't have many trees in

South Africa's desert," his father had said. "That's why I like planting them at home."

A fiery pain stabbed through Ronald's foot. Gasping, he toppled sideways onto the ground, his small arms flailing against his shorts. "No!" he blurted out, his eyes filling with tears. Something was darting away over the dirt — a black, furry thing with crooked legs, fearless as the snakes with tongues that slid across his parents' garden.

Before long, his nurse was upon him, dropping to her knees. Scooping him into her lap, she saw the huge spider waiting slyly atop a bush. "*Tarantula!*" she shrieked, babbling in both English and Afrikaans. "John Ronald Reuel Tolkien! You shouldn't have run off."

The nurse put Ronald on his back under the scorching sun. She lifted his leg upward, grabbed his wounded foot, and pulled it toward the bright red of her mouth. Moaning and cooing, she sucked the spider venom from the swelling beneath his toes. Wincing, Ronald tilted his head so that he could glimpse the base of the camelthorn tree. "Take me to the tree," he said. "I can climb it!"

"I'm taking you home, Master Tolkien! You can rest on the balcony upstairs and look at the trees your father planted."

Carrying him like a large sack of corn, his socks and

shoes bulging from her pockets, the woman awkwardly loped away from the farmland and hurried down a road near her native *kraal,* or village. Ronald's foot stung even more as it touched the starched pleats of her apron; cringing, he imagined spiders crawling out of her hair. At Bloemfontein's market square, not far from his home, he saw houseboys on their daily errands. "May I have an apple?" he asked, his voice trembling, but his nurse bypassed the stalls and ran over the steps of the Raadzaal, Bloemfontein's most important government building.

"Mrs. Tolkien! Mrs. Tolkien!" the nurse called in singsong cadence when, a few moments later, she dashed with Ronald into the Tolkien house. "A tarantula bit your son!"

Mabel Tolkien hurried from the kitchen, her long skirt hoisted above her ankles, her face drawn from the day's excruciating heat. Seeing the crimson welt on the bottom of Ronald's foot, she took him from the nurse's shoulders. "Africa's playground," she whispered sadly to herself, then asked Isaak, the houseboy, for calamine lotion and bandages from the cupboard.

Ronald's foot was swabbed with pink lotion and covered with gauze. "It was a spider as big as a dragon!" he told his mother. He asked to sit on the balcony with his favorite book of fairy tales, the one with pictures of fire-breathing dragons and goblins, but his mother only reluctantly agreed. Always, she fretted over his health, finding him too thin and frail for the relentless sun.

From a balcony chair, Ronald opened the book he could not yet read, caught up by an etching of an armored knight on horseback whose sword menaced a two-headed dragon. Below, in the Tolkien garden, trees planted by Ronald's father — cypresses, firs, and cedars — rustled as if the brave knight had just ridden past them. Ronald stood up, putting his weight squarely on both feet, defiant against the soreness under the gauze. Perhaps, he thought, he was crushing spiders with his feet and might, himself, be a brave knight. He decided he would ask Isaak, the houseboy — not his nurse, who always said "No," or his mother, who often looked sad — to take him back to the desert farm in the morning so that, even with his bandaged tarantula bite, he might finally climb the camelthorn tree.

Ronald had been, from the start, an observant child, quick to mark details around him — the shop signs along Maitland Street; the gray blue of the Indian Ocean, where he once was bathed; the wilting boughs of the eucalyptus tree at his first Christmas. Brought to his father's bank office, he would find pencils and paper and make simple drawings of what he'd seen. He drew the locusts that had descended on the dry grassland

and destroyed the harvests. He drew the ox wagons that carried bales of wool into the market square, and the white two-story house where he lived with his parents, Arthur and Mabel Tolkien, and his one-year-old brother, Hilary.

Born and raised in England, his parents had moved to Africa to begin their marriage. At Lloyds Bank in Birmingham, England, his father's salary had been too small to support a family; he'd gone to Bloemfontein when offered a better job by the Bank of Africa. His mother — homesick before she'd even left England's shores — had followed in April 1891, her steamer trunk full of Birmingham mementos.

On an April day four years later, weeks after Ronald was bitten by the tarantula, he climbed onto the family steamer trunk in the parlor, touching its dented corners and polished lid. His mother had been packing the trunk with clothes; she'd told him that he and Hilary would be traveling with her to visit relatives in faraway England. "You'll be much cooler while we're away," his mother said, "and you'll grow fatter. How long I've waited for this trip! If only your father could come with us."

Talk in the household was that Arthur Tolkien was too busy at the bank to be given "home leave." Traders and miners were making new investments from South Africa's gold and diamond strikes and from the railroad that connected the cities of Cape Town and Johannes-burg. Ronald's father had been promoted to branch manager at the bank, yet he would earn only half-pay if he took leave.

Ronald was soon discovered on top of the trunk. His father, dressed in one of the white suits he wore to work, carried a small jar of paint and a tapered brush into the parlor. "Sit on the rug," his father said gently. "You can watch me label the trunk so it won't be lost on your jour-ney."

Opening the jar, Arthur Tolkien smiled at his son and dipped the brush into the black paint. Carefully, he stooped down and began painting letters across the trunk lid. Ronald stared at the line of shapes he longed to know how to read; they seemed to him as magical as the fairy-tale pictures in his book. His parents could read words, as could the clerks at his father's office. Words and trees — and knights and dragons — were what Ronald wanted. "I've written my name," his father said, straightening up with a pride Ronald would always remember. "A. R. TOLKIEN. Arthur Reuel Tolkien. You also carry the name Reuel."

Six days later, dressed in their finest outfits and hav-ing traveled by carriage and railroad car, Ronald, his mother, and Hilary boarded the ship SS *Guelph* at Cape Town's harbor. The ocean voyage would require three weeks; Jane Suffield, Mabel Tolkien's younger sister, would meet them at the wharf in the city of Southampton, England.

On shipboard, startled by the vastness around him, Ronald watched the blue waves of the Atlantic Ocean. In the distance, the lighter blue of the sky seemed to curve downward on all sides toward the water — like the bell jar he'd seen with Isaak in a Bloemfontein shopwindow. He tried to imagine his bedroom curtains at home and the wicker chair in the garden. He tried, squinting his eyes, to see the trees his father had planted — trees that had been his friends. Why were his room and the garden so far away? If he couldn't see them, were they still real? If he could only imagine the place called England, was it a fairy tale from his book?

Feeling the deck swaying and rocking beneath him, Ronald closed his fingers around the lower ship rail. His mother stood beside him, holding Hilary, the puffed sleeves of her blouse billowing in the wind. Ronald tried as hard as he could to think of his father — to make him appear at the rail. He could almost see the white suit and mustache, even while they slipped away in the wind. Mostly, though, he could see the shiny black letters his father had painted across the trunk lid: A. R. TOLKIEN. The name took shape like one of the signs on Maitland Street, soothing an ache inside Ronald's chest.

He leaned sideways then into the deep folds of his mother's skirt. His father had said that if the bank work grew quieter, he might join the family in England. Or, if not, he would await their return. Ronald didn't understand why missing his father suddenly frightened him — like a goblin's great fangs coming closer. He would send his father a pencil drawing from England that could be tacked onto the bank office wall, and he would ask his father to write back a letter. Then everything would be fine.

But as the wind skittered and howled over the deck and the ship moved on its course away from South Africa, Ronald clung to his memory of the magic letters: A. R. TOLKIEN. The letters, somehow, had become his father, for it seemed to Ronald — in a dark premonition far beyond his years — that he would never see his father again.

Chapter 2

IN THE SUFFIELDS' SMALL HOUSE in the King's Heath suburb of Birmingham, something was always happening. Ronald's grandfather told jokes, making his grandmother and his uncle Willie laugh. His aunt Jane sat for hours on the stairs, listening to the young man, the lodger, play banjo. Summer days in England became autumn, then winter. Ronald's father kept hoping to make the voyage, but work detained him. By December, when Ronald was indeed a bit fatter, he longed to show his father the Christmas tree in the Suffield parlor. The tree, like himself, was not as skinny and frail as the African eucalyptus.

On Sundays, the family walked to an Anglican church. The sight of the hymnal words was far more beautiful to Ronald than the sounds of the organ or the choir. After the sermon, he would wait for his mother in a vestibule among the parishioners, instructed not to let go of Hilary's hand. Outside, in the street, carriages rolled by, buffed and shining. No knights, however — like the ones from his old book of fairy tales — were astride the horses; no dragons breathed fire in the morning light.

One snowy day, a wrinkled letter arrived from Bloemfontein, turning Mabel Tolkien's cheeks an ashen white. Ronald's father had contracted rheumatic fever; he was being treated by a doctor for pains in his chest and legs. Mabel almost booked return passage to Africa on the next ship, but Arthur wrote that he was already feeling better.

"Is Papa too sick to come to us?" Ronald asked.

"For now," his mother told him. "Yet he says he is much improved."

The banjo songs grew somber as winter deepened and letters arrived less frequently from Bloemfontein. Finally, in late January, word came that Arthur was desperately ill. Mabel packed the steamer trunk, her eyes moist with tears. Tracing a finger over the painted lettering on the lid, Ronald said aloud what he still could not read: "A. R. TOLKIEN. A. R. TOLKIEN."

A hurried message, dictated by Ronald in his most grownup voice, was to be dispatched to his father, saying that the family was sailing home — that Ronald had grown to be "such a big man." Before the note could be posted, however, a telegram was delivered: Arthur Tolkien, thirty-nine years old, had suffered a hemorrhage. By the next day, February 15, 1896, Mabel learned that her husband was dead.

The grief that struck the Suffields in King's Heath descended, also, on the Tolkien family in Birmingham. John Benjamin Tolkien, Arthur's father, was so devastated by his son's death that within six months he, too, would die. Ronald had visited his grandfather Tolkien and his aunt Grace Tolkien during his stay in England, but the Suffields were more familiar to him. Now, in the wake of tragedy, his aunt Grace told him tales about Tolkien ancestors, of how they'd settled in London in the early 1800s, skilled at piano making and at manufacturing clocks.

Arthur Tolkien was buried before his family could sail for Africa, making the trip unnecessary. He had left little money. Mabel, planning never again to leave England, would have only thirty shillings a week for herself and the children, not enough for even meager quarters. Her parents urged her to stay on with them, but she wanted to make her own way. At last, when a Suffield relative provided extra funds, she searched newspaper ads for cheap but decent rentals in the country, away from the smokestacks and soot of Birmingham. In summer, she found a tiny brick cottage in the hamlet of Sarehole, several miles from her parents' home.

Sarehole, with its quiet meadows and streams, its cascade of trees and flowers, would be a haven for Ronald. As much as he loved the Suffields, he'd been anxious and fearful since his father's death. The dragons he'd once loved to think about had become threatening to him. Somehow, he felt safe in Sarehole. With Hilary in hand, he would dart through the gate of the rented cottage, up a hill, and over a road to where tall willows ribboned the River Cole. Leaning against a tree trunk or climbing onto broad, tangled limbs, he would call to Hilary, who hunted in the dirt for corn-cockle weeds. "Don't go near the water," he'd warn his brother, alert now to possible dangers.

By the spring of 1897, when Ronald was five, his mother — fluent in Latin, French, and German as well as English — taught him to read in all four languages. Encouraging his love for plants and trees, she introduced him to the science of botany. He experimented with drawing leaves, stems, and blossoms, giving shape on paper to what he'd seen in the meadows. As he and Hilary traipsed through the fields, he would name aloud the various flowers and plants, explaining their parts and functions to his younger brother.

Near the River Cole stood Sarehole's old mill, where corn had been ground until 1698, when the steam engine was invented. Now the mill was used for grinding bones to make fertilizer. Transfixed, Ronald and Hilary would watch the huge waterwheel turn in its dark pit, or they would sneak past the mill gate where, through an open doorway, they could stare at webs of leather belts on heavy pulleys and shafts. A mill worker, covered from head to foot with white bone dust, always yelled at the boys to get away from the doorway. Ronald called him the White Ogre — choosing the name Black Ogre for the mean-faced farmer on the hill, who chased him for picking mushrooms and who was said to whip country boys.

One afternoon, while Hilary napped in the cottage, Ronald took off alone. At a narrow sandpit, he rolled pebbles down the slopes; at a mossy pool, he beckoned to the swans. A farm cart was rattling by when he found a tantalizing patch of brown mushrooms. His heart pounding, he remembered the word his mother had taught him for mushrooms that could be eaten: *Agaricus*. Turning slowly in a circle, he saw no one near him. Though he wasn't hungry, he wanted to pick the mushrooms, even if — or *especially* if — the Black Ogre caught him. The mushrooms would be his treasure; without armor, horse, or sword, he would escape with them!

Plucking the stalks, careful not to rip the caplike tops, Ronald stuffed mushrooms into his pockets and down the front of his shirt. He would, he thought, offer them to his mother. They might make her smile, something rare and wondrous since his father had died. Busy at his task, he didn't notice another farm cart on the hill — or the tall, gangly figure in stained overalls who lurched awkwardly toward him. Only when a gruff voice cut the air, startling him, did he drop a handful of mushrooms. "Caught ya! Stealing food again, you little snot! I'll throttle you black and blue!"

Ronald ran, a delicious kind of terror rising in him. He raced over Sarehole's flowered fields, past the swans in the pond, beside the pebbled sandpit. Gasping for breath, glancing over his shoulder as the Black Ogre shook a fist at him, he ran as fast as he could — faster than he'd run from his nurse in Bloemfontein. He was headed for the road to the rented cottage when he veered sideways. The Black Ogre, he warned himself, would follow him home. His mother would be upset. She wouldn't want mushrooms.

At a grove of trees, Ronald dove between trunks and dipping branches, looking for shelter. Zigzagging as he ran, his shoes slapped against moist, moss-covered earth, and he saw a tree limb reach out like an arm. Grabbing it with both hands, he pulled himself upward, scrambled along the bark on his stomach, then climbed a higher limb, and then one even higher. Leaves brushed silkily against his face, calming him. The tree seemed to take him in, hide him from danger.

Crouched behind leafy branches, his treasure safe in his pockets and inside his shirt, Ronald heard the Black Ogre thunder past, rasping in a cracked voice, "Where are you, little snot?" Ronald knew he would not be discovered — that, at least for the afternoon, the trees had helped him outwit what was mean and frightening. The trees, whether in Bloemfontein, King's Heath, or his beloved Sarehole, were always his friends.

At the age of seven, Ronald took entrance exams at King Edward VI School in Birmingham, where his father had been a student. He did not pass, however, and his mother broadened her tutoring. His reading was not something that needed work. He'd read Hans Christian Andersen, Lewis Carroll, and William Morris. Curious about bows and arrows, he'd devoured Indian stories; and still fascinated by dragons and goblins, he'd followed the adventures in George Macdonald's sagas. His favorite tales were by Andrew Lang, especially the *Red Fairy Book* stories of the heroic Sigurd, who slew Fafnir the dragon. "I desired dragons," Ronald would later say, remembering both his wonderment and fear, "with a profound desire."

In autumn of 1899, Ronald wrote his own dragon story, showing it to his mother. One of her comments would linger with him for the rest of his life, deepening his love of words. He had described "a green great dragon" in his story; the proper word order, his mother had said (though he never stopped wondering why), was "a great green dragon."

Several months before his eighth birthday, Ronald passed the King Edward's exams. A Tolkien uncle offered to pay his school fees. His mother dressed him in a short black velvet coat and knee-length trousers, setting him apart from the other Sarehole boys. He couldn't sneak off to spy on the White Ogre; mill dust would dirty him. Nor could he taunt the Black Ogre by filching mushrooms; stains would ruin his clothes. But he wouldn't stop climbing a tree or two, using his mother's scissors to snip off, in secret, the snags on his trousers.

Attending school in Birmingham meant walking partway for nearly four miles. Mabel Tolkien couldn't afford to send Ronald by train. When his classes began in September 1900, Mabel walked the route with him at first, showing him where he could board the horse-drawn tram. Soon, he insisted on walking alone. At day's end, he'd ignore the aching in his legs. Besides, Hilary would meet him at the cottage gate with a lighted lantern, his small face aglow in the shadows.

King Edward's, the oldest and best boys' school in Birmingham, was a dreary-looking building overlooking New Street train station. Steam and soot streaked the school windows; classroom instruction was muffled by the grinding and shrieking of wheels and whistles. Ronald, used to the quiet of Sarehole, found himself among hundreds of noisy, wisecracking boys, who pressed and shoved down the corridors. He grew accustomed to the school and the chimney smoke, but during his first winter, he was often absent with coughs, too exhausted to walk the four miles back and forth to the tram.

One Wednesday, trudging up the road to the cottage at sunset, he felt feverish and dizzy. He sat down on a wide boulder, letting his schoolbooks fall to his feet. The scent of meadow grass lay like a blanket beneath him. Nearby, a rabbit popped up from a hole, wrinkling its nose. Ronald wanted to lie down and cool his face on the grass. He knew he must go home, that his mother would be worried, but his feet were sore and his legs were shaking. He slid off the boulder to the ground and turned onto his side. Bird sounds were a lullaby, murmuring through the air.

Over an hour had passed when Ronald felt a hand on his forehead. Stirring, he saw his mother's face above him, tears streaking her cheeks. "What?" he asked. "Where am I?"

"Oh, Ronald," his mother sobbed. "I didn't know what had happened. You're burning with fever."

Struggling to his feet, he brushed himself off and picked up his books. "I fell asleep," he said.

As they walked up the road, Mabel Tolkien began talking of what had been on her mind. "I know you love Sarehole, that it has been good for you since your father's death. But you need to live closer to school so you won't be sick. We're moving again, Ronald. I've rented a house on Moseley Street, nearer King Edward's, and right on the tram route."

He stopped walking, as if a dark ocean wave had struck him. He had been moved from South Africa's desert to the greener soil of England — but it was only Sarehole that seemed now like home. The cottages, the flowered dells, and — yes! — the trees had made him happy. He didn't want the belching factories of a city, its noisiness and grime.

"Why does everything change, Mama?" he asked, his own eyes wet with tears. "Why can't things stay the same?"

"Struggle and change give us strength, Ronald," his mother answered. "Think of the mighty Sigurd as he challenged the dragon Fafnir."

Up ahead, Ronald caught sight of Hilary, the lighted

lantern swinging from his brother's hand. Their father was gone, and soon Sarehole would not be theirs. But as Ronald was hurried into the cottage, bundled into bed, and given hot tea, he did try imagining Sigurd. Because of Sigurd, the powerful Fafnir was vanquished and slain. Courage against fear, Ronald thought sleepily — and against Black Ogres, White Ogres, goblins, and dragons — was not just in the pages of fairy tales.

Chapter 3

ONE RENTED HOUSE GAVE WAY to another. No sooner had Mabel settled the children into the ramshackle house on Moseley Street than city officials condemned it. The family moved to a little row house backed onto railroad tracks and a coal yard. Ronald could feel the rooms shake when a train roared by. Missing Sarehole terribly, he would gaze through his bedroom window at the dingy street, imagining the willow trees over the River Cole.

A few flowers and plants grew beside the rails, badges of beauty amidst the grime. Ronald's best find, however, was the collection of coal trucks in the gravel yard. Painted on them, black as his father's lettering on the steamer trunk lid, were strange and fascinating names in the Welsh language: NANTYGLO, BLAEN-RHONDDA, SENGHENYDD, PENRHIWCEIBER. Learning the names, he would say them aloud.

Welsh sounded ancient to him, and more exciting than what he already knew of Latin, German, and French.

It was Latin that he heard in the church his mother now attended. Against the wishes of all her relatives, seeking solace from her loneliness as a widow, she had left the Anglican Church of England to become a Catholic. Ronald had overheard angry outbursts from his Suffield grandparents. The Suffields, his grandfather had said, were solidly Protestant. The Tolkiens were Baptist, Methodist, and Unitarian. Birmingham itself, in spite of growing numbers of Catholic immigrants, was traditionally anti-Catholic. But Mabel had not listened. She'd instructed her sons in Catholicism even when their Suffield uncle, Walter Incledon, cut off some monetary support.

The Catholic church near the row house hadn't pleased Mabel, so, taking the boys with her, she'd hunted for other churches. In the suburb of Edgbaston, she came upon the Birmingham Oratory, a church run by Oratory priests. Next door, on Oliver Road, near the Grammar School of St. Phillip, was a tiny house that Mabel rented early in 1902. The neighborhood was tainted with drunks and vagrants, but Ronald could attend St. Phillip's for less money than his tuition at King Edward's — and be given a Catholic education.

It was at the Oratory that Ronald met Father Francis Morgan. Half-Spanish and half-Welsh, the silver-haired priest understood the Welsh names that Ronald had memorized from the coal trucks and let the boy borrow books from his private library. Before long, Father Francis was advising Mabel to withdraw her son from St. Phillip's. "He's ahead of his classmates," the priest told her. "He needs better instruction, and King Edward's, though secular, gives him that. He might try for a scholarship."

In the fall of 1903, Ronald returned to King Edward's on a Foundation Scholarship. He studied Greek and, on his own, read Chaucer in its original Middle English, the language of England from the twelfth to the end of the fifteenth century. He read G. K. Chesterton and H. G. Wells, who wrote fantasy, and was captivated by the English legends of King Arthur and the heroic knights of the Round Table. When he wasn't reading at home, he helped his mother tutor Hilary, especially when she was tired, and he made his first communion at church.

Though his studies were going well, dragons seemed to lurk around every corner. In midwinter, Ronald and Hilary caught the measles and whooping cough. Then Hilary had pneumonia. From his sickbed, Ronald taught his mother to play chess, the game he'd learned from an

Oratory clergyman. He worried over her sleepless nights when he and Hilary were ill. How weary she looked when she went to buy medicine or food. "Be careful," he'd tell her, thinking of the drunks outside and wishing he'd lived in the days when armor-clad knights rode into battle to rescue good from evil.

One afternoon, home from school, Ronald found a somber-faced Father Francis in his mother's place. "Your mother has collapsed," the priest said. "She's been taken to the hospital. She sends you her love."

To the shock of everyone who knew her, Mabel was diagnosed as being diabetic. With no insulin available in 1904, the only treatment was rest. Ronald left his books unopened, his homework undone. He wrote notes to his mother, which Father Francis carried to the hospital, but when doctors said that Mabel would not be released for several months, the rented house had to go. Father Francis put dishes and furniture in storage and sent Hilary to stay with his Suffield grandparents. Ronald went to his aunt Jane, who'd married the young man who played the wailing banjo songs when Ronald's father was ill.

By summer, Mabel was ready to come home. Father Francis gathered up the boys and settled the family in two cottage rooms at a country retreat for Oratory clergy. The cottage was already occupied by the local postman and his wife, but the wife welcomed Mabel and her sons, offering to cook for them. The wooded area, Ronald told himself, would heal his mother. He renewed his studies. On the grounds of the retreat, he and Hilary went berry gathering and kite flying with Father Francis — and again Ronald climbed his trees.

Mabel seemed to slowly improve. Color returned to her face, and she drew pictures with Ronald and took both boys to a parade. "Don't fret about me," she'd say when she caught Ronald watching her, but he couldn't miss the lost look that lay in her eyes. One November morning, he couldn't rouse her from beneath her blankets. Racing to find the postman's wife, he begged the woman for help. He waited, shivering, as the cottage filled with priests and a groundskeeper went to notify the Suffields. Wiping away Hilary's tears, Ronald would not leave for school or eat the breakfast prepared for him. "Please fetch a doctor for my mother," he kept saying.

Mabel's condition was identified as a diabetic coma. Ronald sat woodenly by her bed, holding her hand. Beside him, Father Francis waited in the soft light from the cottage window. "She knows you are with her," he heard the priest say.

Six days later, on November 14, 1904 — eight years after her husband's death — Mabel Tolkien died. "We're orphans," Ronald told Hilary. Mabel was buried at the

Catholic cemetery in nearby Bromsgrove, her grave decorated with a stone cross. At her gravesite, surrounded by trees that looked to Ronald as if they were bowing their heads, Suffields and Tolkiens intertwined. Ronald and Hilary were taken aside by Father Francis, who'd been named by their mother as legal guardian. "I'll protect you both," Father Francis said.

Empty, that desolate day, of the words that always seemed so alive to him, twelve-year-old Ronald could barely nod his head in reply. The dragons, hissing fire, were far too strong.

Of all the Suffields and Tolkiens in Birmingham, only one, Beatrice Suffield, was not bent on removing Ronald and Hilary from the Catholic Church. Father Francis talked to aunts, uncles, cousins, and grandparents, seeking proper housing for his charges. Beatrice, an aunt by marriage, who was not much of a churchgoer, lived near the Birmingham Oratory and agreed to take the boys. She provided a room on the top floor of her house on Stirling Road.

At his aunt's, Ronald would awaken most nights from a dream: a huge wave was crashing over the earth, washing everything away. In daylight, when he wasn't at school, he escaped from the dream to the Oratory, serving early morning Mass for Father Francis, eating with Hilary in the refectory, playing with the church cat.

Hilary now attended King Edward's, and the brothers walked together to school or rode the horse bus. They did not tell Father Francis that their aunt Beatrice was gruff with them; they sought, instead, to win her favor.

Whenever Ronald thought of his mother's death, he would try remembering what she had taught him — a love of language and learning, country landscapes and Catholicism, botany and art. Gradually, these loves fused with his memory of his mother and gave him comfort. Shortly after the funeral, he had been taken on holiday by Father Francis, whose Oratorian vows allowed the priest to keep a small family income. They traveled to Wales for Ronald to hear the Welsh language that had so bewitched him; and, in the summer, they visited England's seashore at Lyme Regis, where Mabel Tolkien would have marveled at the unspoiled land.

Ronald's greatest escape was, of course, into books — those he owned or borrowed, those he read at Cornish's Bookshop in Birmingham. At school, his form master, George Brewerton, was so impressed by his ability to read Middle English that he lent Ronald a primer in Anglo-Saxon, or Old English, the language of England before the Norman Conquest of 1066. By the next fall, Ronald could translate long paragraphs of Anglo-Saxon. He read the oldest of all known English poems, *Beowulf* — an eighth-century Old English tale of warrior

Beowulf's clash with monsters and his death after battling a dragon — and he tackled *Sir Gawain and the Green Knight,* a medieval poem about an Arthurian knight who suffers an ax blow at the hands of a giant. Ronald also discovered Gothic and became intrigued by this dead language of the third- and fourth-century Goths.

The headmaster at King Edward's was informed of Ronald's achievements and assigned him to study philology, the science and history of words. By tracking the evolution of words, a philology student could embark on a treasure hunt for principles held in common by languages. Ronald had already begun his own hunt, sneaking from bed each night at his aunt's and, in the moonlit parlor, painstakingly inventing a new language that he called Naffarin. Structuring an entire sound system and grammar, even inventing a history, he kept a diary, writing either in Naffarin or in code symbols he'd devised for the English alphabet.

His aunt Beatrice did not like the discarded pages of strange words filling her trash bags; grumbling to herself, she burned the paper in her fireplace. Several months past his sixteenth birthday, Ronald was devastated to find she had also burned all of his mother's letters, never asking if he'd wanted to keep them. "It's time you move elsewhere," Father Francis said.

On Duchess Road, behind the Oratory, a Mrs. Faulkner ran a boarding house for orphaned children. Adding some of his own funds to the small income from Mabel Tolkien's estate, Father Francis made arrangements for Ronald and Hilary to share a second-floor room. Another orphan, nineteen-year-old Edith Bratt, lived on the first floor, and a maid, Annie, cooked and cleaned.

Ronald was relieved to be living at Mrs. Faulkner's. The house was dingy and dark, but he and Hilary had a fairly large room. Within days of moving, he had made friends with Edith Bratt. Raised by her mother near Birmingham, Edith was slim and quite pretty. She played the piano and sewed on a machine whose sounds hummed through the house. She had hoped to be a concert pianist but had been placed at Mrs. Faulkner's after her mother died. Evenings in the boarding house were often given over to musical presentations attended by Oratory clergy, and Edith played the piano for admiring vocalists and listeners. Though she was three years older than Ronald and he'd not talked much to girls, he felt at ease with her. Even Hilary, only fourteen, sought out her company.

Food was not plentiful at Mrs. Faulkner's, and Ronald, Hilary, and Edith persuaded Annie to smuggle them extra snacks. They concocted whistle signals between them, one of which warned of "impending danger" if Mrs. Faulkner was near. One evening, while the land-lady dozed, Edith wheedled a whole bag of sugar cookies from Annie. Ronald and Hilary were up in their room, poised to carry out the next step of the plan.

From his window, Ronald lowered a rope over the bricks of the house to the open window of the down-stairs pantry, where Edith was waiting. The thick hemp rope skipped and dangled over the pantry windowsill. Clutching at the rope's frayed end, Edith yanked it to-ward her and, fingers flying, tied it around the cookie bag. When she signaled Ronald, he began tugging up-ward, with Hilary calling, "Onward, soldiers!" In the pantry, Edith couldn't stop grinning. But just as the bag was in reach of Ronald's hand, wobbling only a foot away in the air, he heard Edith whistle the danger signal. Star-tled, he glanced downward. Cupping the dark crown of Edith's head was Mrs. Faulkner's gnarled hand. "What are you doing, Missy?" he heard the landlady say. "You'll be chilled."

Aware that Mrs. Faulkner might catch the trio at their mischief, Ronald pulled so quickly at the rope and its bounty that, in a single lurch, he fell backward — and out of sight — onto the floor of his room. Rubbing a scraped elbow while Hilary helped him to his feet, he felt happier than he had in a long time. Whether the cookie prank reminded him of Sarehole's Black Ogre and the pilfered mushrooms or whether he was imagining eating a treasure of warm cookies, he was suddenly glad that, in a world of unexpected turns of light and darkness, Edith Bratt had become his friend.

Chapter 4

BY THE SUMMER OF 1909, Ronald and Edith were in love. That Edith was an "older woman" and a Protestant did not deter them. With his final year approaching at King Edward's, Ronald was to study for a scholarship to Oxford University, the finest educational institution in England — but the year was full of distractions. At first, it was playing rugby football with a school friend, Christopher Wiseman; then he'd joined the Debating Society, amazing his classmates with debates in Greek, Gothic, and Anglo-Saxon. But it was Edith who truly took his mind off his studies. They often talked together far into the night from their first- and second-floor windows.

Both of them knew their relationship could cause a scandal. Not only did they live in the same house, but Ronald was only seventeen. Deciding to meet in secret, they planned a bicycle ride in the country. To anyone who asked, Edith said she was biking to visit her cousin Jennie Grove. Ronald claimed he was off to the sports field for rugby practice. He and Edith spent a clandestine afternoon biking near the village of Rednal, later stopping for tea. Back at Mrs. Faulkner's, they were pleased over their adventure — until, two days later, Father Francis confronted Ronald at the Oratory.

"I've received shocking news," the priest said. "My cook tells me of gossip from a woman in Rednal: you and Edith Bratt were seen together, laughing and quite affectionate. The girl is three years your senior, Ronald! You need to study for a scholarship, not waste time. The relationship with Miss Bratt must stop at once! I will find new quarters for you and Hilary."

Ronald was quiet in the face of Father Francis's anger. He had great affection for his guardian and felt he owed him respect. He also knew he couldn't afford to live in Birmingham without the priest's assistance. Accepting the move with Hilary to another boarding house, Ronald tried to be diligent about studying, but he still met Edith in secret. When he finally went to Oxford for his entrance exams, he hoped to justify his romance by winning a fine scholarship. He was thrilled by his first view of the stately colleges and chapels of the University. He found, on tree-lined Merton Street, Brasenose Lane, and Radcliffe Square, classical and literary knowledge unparalleled in other cities.

After returning to Birmingham, Ronald waited for an official letter of notification. Its contents, however, would surprise and dismay him. He had no triumph to bring to Edith or Father Francis; in the face of fierce student competition and his own lack of preparation, he had failed to win an award. The exams would be repeated in December, but if he didn't succeed then, he could not attend the University on scholarship. He knew neither Father Francis nor his Suffield and Tolkien relatives could afford the fees. Depressed, he wrote in English, not Naffarin, in his diary. He was "in the dark," he said. He must study harder. He asked for God's help.

He could not, however, stop seeing Edith. They planned another outing, mulling over arrangements. Taking the train to a distant suburb where no one knew them, they shopped and ate on a back street. At a jeweler's, Edith bought Ronald a pen for his eighteenth birthday; he bought her a wristwatch for her twenty-first. Under an awning, she suddenly took his arm. "I'm going to Cheltenham," she told him. "Mr. and Mrs. Jessop, whom I've known for years, invited me to live with them." Then, seeing Ronald's pained expression, Edith added, "You and I can write each other. You'll study better when I'm gone."

"How?" he asked her. "Missing you will fill my thoughts."

Whether it was fate or the ominous dragons, Ronald and Edith were observed again by someone from the Oratory. This time, Father Francis was irate. "ENOUGH!" the priest boomed at Ronald, ordering him not to see Edith or even to write her letters. Though he could bid her goodbye on the day she left for Cheltenham, he must have absolutely no further contact with her until his twenty-first birthday — a wait of three years.

Ronald left the Oratory in a daze. He wandered across Birmingham, stopping at sundown to stare from a safe distance at Edith's window. A week passed before he saw her by accident in a courtyard, and he squeezed her hand in relief. Two days later, they spoke briefly when he passed her on the street. Her small frame was hunched against the wind, and she seemed to Ronald as unprotected as his mother had been among the vagrants on Oliver Road. That night, he wrote in his diary that Edith had been "coming from the Cathedral to pray for me."

Three days following this brief encounter, a "dreadful letter" arrived for Ronald from Father Francis. Somehow, beyond rational explanation, the priest had learned of the street meeting, presuming it was planned. Calling it foolhardy and evil, Father Francis threatened to withdraw all support for Ronald's future unless he completely cut Edith from his life for three years. Shaken, Ronald did not know what to do. He had given his word to Father Francis that he would obey him. Honor and loyalty were at stake.

On the day of Edith's departure — March 2, 1910 — Ronald wanted to catch a last glimpse of her. He stood stiffly on the icy road to the train station, regretting nothing he had done, certain that Edith was his good fortune. At the corner of St. Francis Road, he finally saw her — her coat wrapped around her legs, her scarf blowing against her shoulders as she bicycled toward the station.

Tempted as he was to step forward, to call out Edith's name and promise, somehow, to contact her, he stayed rooted, like one of his trees, to the ground. "I shall not," he would write in anguish in his diary, "see her again perhaps for three years."

Keeping busy was the best medicine. He completed his work for senior year and studied for his second chance at the Oxford exams. On late afternoons, he, Christopher Wiseman, and another King Edward's student, R. Q. Gilson, met over tea at the school library, talking and reading from favorite essays and tales. For amusement, they called themselves the Tea Club. When cleanup crews arrived at the library, pouring sawdust over the floors and sweeping it up into buckets, Ronald — called John Ronald or Tolkien by his friends — would toss all the used tea leaves into the sawdust.

By summer, a fourth schoolmate, G. B. Smith, had joined the club. Meetings were held at Barrow's Stores, a restaurant on Corporation Street. The Tea Club became the Barrovian Society, though both names were linked together as initials: T.C.B.S. Leaning across wooden tables, the four friends read aloud from Latin and Greek literature, modern classics, and poetry. Ronald brought Norse tales to the group and recited from *Beowulf* or *Sir Gawain and the Green Knight*. He was writing verse, inspired by the fairy spirits and elves of the mystic poetry of Francis Thompson. Putting aside, for the moment, his fascination with dragons, monsters, and knights of battle, he invoked in his rhymes the "sprites of the wood," asking them to sing to him before they might fade from sight.

Permitted one last letter to Edith by Father Francis, Ronald wrote her a fervent note and heard from her in return. She sent him her love, saying she was playing piano for an Anglican church in Cheltenham and taking organ lessons. He reread her words hundreds of times, keeping the letter inside his pants pocket. Bicycling home from rugby practice to his room, he could hear the soft crinkling of the folded paper.

In December, he boarded the train to Oxford, where the University was made up of separate colleges, each in its own building. Walking past an ancient iron cross on Broad Street, he was the only young man not wearing the University's traditional black gown. He was, of course, an outsider who'd come for exams — not yet a "tosher," the derogatory Oxford term for students from working-class backgrounds. At the end of the grueling day, he bought a map of the town. Oxford had been fortified by great walls during the Middle Ages but was now surrounded by fields and villages, free of the smoking factories and dank slums of Birmingham. Horse-drawn trams and bicycles were still the usual transportation, but several motorcars churned past him, noisy creations of a man named Morris, who owned a bicycle repair shop on High Street.

Back in Birmingham, Ronald waited again for the notification letter. He worried over his meager finances; so many Oxford students were wealthy, belonging to University clubs and societies, indulging in fox hunting, steeplechasing, and weekend parties in London or Paris. At moments, he envied them: They had bought their way into Oxford, even with poor grades.

This time, the official Oxford letter brought him good news. Though he'd not been awarded the highest possible scholarship, he had outscored all competitors for a slightly lower Exhibition award at the University's Exeter College. "Your mother would be proud," Father Francis told him. "You could have done even better — but your mind is clearing of dust."

In June, Ronald graduated from King Edward VI School and realized he would miss its easy familiarity. He wrote in his diary that without either Edith or King Edward's, he was "like a young sparrow kicked out of a high nest." Even his brother was gone, having dropped out of school to study architecture and work on a farm. At Cornish's bookstore, Ronald turned to the nineteenth-century poetry of the Finnish myths in *Kalevala*, or *Land of Heroes*, losing himself for hours in "this strange people and these new gods."

Late in the month, he went on a walking tour in Switzerland, organized by the farm family who employed Hilary. The small group of twelve carried heavy backpacks, keeping off Switzerland's main roads and climbing glaciers and mountain paths. At night, straw huts or haylofts served as shelter. On a snowy incline of the Aletsch Glacier, Ronald and Hilary were using walking sticks when, under the burn of summer sun, they felt loose rocks beneath their feet. They suddenly heard a deep rumbling above them — boulders began to roll off the glacier, gathering speed in their descent. "Take care,

Hilary!", Ronald called out, as he'd once called to his brother near the pond in Sarehole.

Zigzagging in the avalanche, the boulders plunged downward, dozens of them disappearing into the ravines. Any one of them could have crushed a tour member, causing instant death. Ronald, his heart pounding louder in his ears than the pound of rocks on snow, tried not to trip as he darted to one side. Was this to be his own end, he wondered — a cold grave in Switzerland to follow his father's grave in Africa and his mother's in England?

A boulder careened past him, a foot from his head. Everyone scattered, running in circles, gasping under the onslaught of stone. Fifteen minutes passed before the rumbling quieted, leaving Ronald and Hilary together under blue sky and white snow. Only later, after the ragged tour members slowly climbed down the glacier to the warmth of a small chalet inn, did Ronald recall that just before the boulder almost hit him, he'd reached for Edith's letter, still folded inside his pocket. He would never stop believing it was the letter that had kept him from harm's way.

Chapter 5

THE WINDOW OF HIS ROOM at Exeter College looked down on Turl Street, nestled in the oldest section of Oxford. Next door, in the small garden between Exeter and the Divinity School, a silver birch tree and several horse chestnuts reached upward, a call to sun and sky. Ronald could take a refreshing walk among the trees yet be only minutes away from the Bodleian Libraries, the History of Science Museum, and the Sheldonian Theatre.

Beneath the staircase in Exeter's foyer was a board with the names of the sixty male students. Women were in separate colleges on the outskirts of town. Seeing his name, Ronald would ask himself if he was *really* at Oxford. Since English tradition favored the use of last names over first, "Tolkien" or "J.R.R. Tolkien" was his identity to both professors and students. He began now to feel an even closer link to his father's lettering across the steamer trunk lid.

So it was as Tolkien that he signed up for the Honors Program in Classics, that he joined the Debating Society and the Essay Club, and that — tall, lean, and quite handsome now at age nineteen — he was chosen to play on the baseball and cricket teams. Though he longed for Edith, wondering how he could ever wait until he was twenty-one to see her, he told no one at Oxford about her. Whenever loneliness gripped him, he kept it to himself.

He would be assigned, over the next four years, to study with a distinguished array of teachers and tutors. Professor Joseph Wright, who'd worked in a woolen mill at age six and later wrote the *English Dialect Dictionary* and a Gothic primer, would teach him Comparative Philology. Professor William Craigie, a world-famous philologist and one of four editors of the *Oxford English Dictionary*, would introduce him to Icelandic mythology. And Professor Kenneth Sisam, a New Zealander specializing in fourteenth-century literature, would inspire him to learn the West Midland dialect of Middle English, spoken by Mabel Tolkien's ancestors.

Attending Oxford, however, meant more than just serious study. Ronald was no longer under the watchful eye of Father Francis. If he skipped a lecture or two, perhaps on Cicero or Demosthenes, if he was lazy about homework or didn't appear at Sunday Mass, he was not reprimanded. He might work, instead, on his new invented language, Quenya, or stop for coffee at Buols café. One of his friends from the T.C.B.S., G. B. Smith, was at Oxford, and the two often met at Swains pub or made the rounds of some of the men's colleges: All Souls, Brasenose, Corpus Christi, Hartford, Balliol, or Merton.

"Ragging," or hazing, of new students by upperclassmen was common at Oxford. At Balliol College, filled with wealthy young men, Ronald was labeled Poor Orphan Tolkien. New students like Ronald were also subjected to "progging" if they misbehaved: a senior upperclassman, assisted by two muscular, bowler-hatted "bulldogs," roamed the streets announcing their names. One evening, when Edith seemed especially far away, Ronald joined a noisy street mix of unruly "gownies" (students in their gowns) and "townies" (young people not attending the University). Beer steins were held aloft and snide remarks hurled back and forth. Ronald and G. B. Smith "captured" a bus, driving it to Cornmarket Street with a rowdy crowd of laughing and shrieking gownies and townies. Fortunately, he and Smith escaped progging or any punishment by the Oxford faculty or police.

Most of Ronald's holidays from Exeter were spent in Birmingham with relatives and Father Francis, or in nearby Barnt Green with an uncle and aunt. He was always short of money and could not travel with friends, but one holiday he joined a cavalry regiment camp, King Edward's Horse, and rode over the plains near Folkestone. He recounted many of his experiences on the trip in his diary; since he was still forbidden to write *to* Edith, he found comfort in writing *for* her.

In 1913, when he finally approached his twenty-first birthday, Ronald was a second-year student at Oxford. The ban on his romance with Edith was nearing its end. He had met Father Francis's demands; he had not seen Edith or contacted her — but contrary to the priest's hopes, neither had he forgotten her. On the night of January 2, just hours before his birthday, he sat in his room at Exeter, turning pages of philology books with a feeling of exultation. Watching the clock hands move toward midnight, he tried to calm himself by reciting two lines by Cynewulf, an Anglo-Saxon poet of the ninth century:

> *"Éala Éarendel engla beorhtast*
> *ofer middangeard monnum sended."*

(Hail Éarendel, brightest of angels
above the middle-earth sent unto men.)

Edith, he felt, was his own "brightest of angels," his Éarendel star marking the dawn. Soon, that dawn would arrive, and Edith would be more than in his thoughts. He had decided he would become a poet for her, using his invented languages, Naffarin and Quenya, to lend "music" to his poems.

At the stroke of midnight, he reached for pen and paper. Words poured from him. He told Edith that he loved her, that they were free now to marry, to join together "before God and the world." When he'd sealed his letter in an envelope, he bolted down the stairs. Mail was not collected until daylight, but he wanted to be sure that his marriage proposal was in the receptacle. Someone at the front door wisecracked at him, "Isn't this past your bedtime, Tolkien?" but he didn't answer.

For the next two weeks, he painstakingly checked the return mail, searching for Edith's reply. When it came, however, it ripped the air from his lungs. Twenty-four-year-old Edith was not in any position, she wrote, to think of marrying him; in fact, she was engaged to a man named George Field, the brother of an old friend. Standing on the stair landing, Edith's letter held in trembling hands, Ronald couldn't believe that Éarendel's dawn had unexpectedly turned black.

Ronald chose to plunge into battle with a sword of words. Writing again, he told Edith that he was taking the train to Cheltenham and must see her. On Wednesday, January 8, she met him on the train platform, her brown hair upswept, her face solemn. "Hello, Ronald," she said, and he thought his heart would break.

They walked for an hour into the country, then sat under a railway viaduct for the rest of the day. Whatever debating skills Ronald had gained were put to full use. When Edith admitted that she thought he had "ceased to care," he exploded in a whirlwind of words, convincing her otherwise. When she balked at breaking her engagement, wary of hurting George Field and his family, Ronald spoke of a greater duty to one's heart. By day's end, Edith had promised to return her engagement ring; she would marry Ronald Tolkien.

They agreed to postpone announcing the betrothal. "Your relatives," Ronald said, "won't approve of an orphaned, penniless Catholic who intends to write poetry in the ancient tradition of Old English, Celtic, and Icelandic bards. I should at least have the prospect of an Oxford teaching post in Classics or Philology. Also, I must write Father Francis about my plans."

A letter from Ronald was soon dispatched to the Birmingham Oratory. Father Francis sent back a resigned reply. By then, Edith had been persuaded by Ronald to convert to Catholicism. Her Protestant friends would turn their backs on her, and she would have to give up her organist post at Cheltenham's Anglican church, but Ronald reminded her that his own mother had endured such hardships.

He tried to remind *himself* to study for his Honour Moderations, the first of two exams, and he submitted papers toward his Classics degree. Three months later, after the Moderations were completed, he was awarded Second Class Honours, comparable to a B grade. While he was disappointed that he hadn't managed a First Class, his paper on Comparative Philology was marked "pure alpha," virtually perfect, and he knew that Edith was finally his.

He began writing poetry and stories in Quenya and was tracking down the origins of certain Old English, Icelandic, and Indo-European, or Germanic, words. Philology breathed life for him into the "bones" of old writings, providing a pathway to ancient and hidden facts. Skillful readers, Ronald discovered, could actually *feel* some of the history behind words, as if the sounds and style of a language offered clues about those who once spoke it. He was convinced philology might lead to the mythology of a people, those colorful stories of creation, gods, and men, of creatures and other designs of nature, of conquests and crusades.

Ronald wrote a poem in English about Cynewulf's Éarendel as an evening, not a morning, star. In the poem, Éarendel makes a grand voyage as a starship across the night sky, fading from sight as morning comes. The first verse of the poem, showing an impressive mastery of rhyme and rhythm, was Ronald's first step at actually creating mythology:

> *Éarendel sprang up from the Ocean's cup*
> *In the gloom of the mid-world's rim;*
> *From the door of Night as a ray of light*
> *Leapt over the twilight brim,*
> *And launching his bark like a silver spark*
> *From the golden-fading sand*
> *Down the sunlit breath of Day's fiery death*
> *He sped from Westerland.*

With his degree in Classics in sight, Ronald decided — after receiving consent from his tutors — to forgo the immediate degree and switch his major study field to English Language and Literature, a way of digging deeper into philology. He'd won the Skeat Prize for English, spending part of the award money on fantasy tales by William Morris, who had graduated from Exeter. Morris, influenced by Icelandic mythology, wrote in great detail about the ancient forest of Mirkwood, where Ronald could easily imagine, from his childhood readings of Andrew Lang, battles between his old favorites, Sigurd and the dragon Fafnir.

In January 1914, Edith was received into the Roman Catholic Church. She had moved to the city of Warwick with Jennie Grove, the cousin she'd once "visited" when she and Ronald had sneaked off on bicycles. Unwilling to wait any longer, the couple was officially betrothed in Warwick's Catholic church where, to Ronald's delight, Edith made her first confession and Communion. Yet when he visited Warwick on weekends, he and Edith often argued. Not only did they need to get to know each other again, but there was an added tension: War talk had been rumbling between England and Germany, and Edith was afraid that if war broke out, she'd lose Ronald forever.

World War I began in August. Allied troops, including Russia, France, Great Britain, Japan, and, later, the United States, were pitted against the Central Powers — Germany, Austria-Hungary, Bulgaria, and Turkey. With thousands of Oxford students enlisting in England's army, the colleges served partially as barracks. Army drills filled the parks and marching bands packed the streets. Ronald wanted to earn his degree before joining the army. He'd signed up for practice drills with a local Officers' Training Corps, so he was able to keep taking classes. How could he ever marry Edith, he asked himself, if he went off to war without a degree?

By 1915, student enrollment at Oxford had dropped from three thousand to one thousand; few able-bodied young men were left in town. The English army had suffered huge losses in France, Belgium, and Turkey. Italians were being massacred by Austrians, Prussians had attacked Russians, and poisonous gas was being used on the Western Front. As the list of dead Oxford students kept mounting, the colleges became hospital way stations.

In an empty cubicle at Exeter, while moans from wounded soldiers echoed nearby, Ronald took his final exams in English Language and Literature. His stomach churned over not being in uniform. When he was awarded First Class Honours — and, at last, his degree — he went immediately to the military office, asking to be posted to the Nineteenth Battalion of the Lancashire Fusiliers, where his friend G. B. Smith was commissioned. Then he took a train to Warwick, where he met Edith on the platform. Holding her hand, he carefully told her of his First-Class award and of the Lancashire Fusiliers.

"But when will we marry?" Edith asked sadly.

"I may not survive the war," he answered. "If we are man and wife, you'd be a widow — like my mother."

Her eyes fluttered closed. "I'm tired of waiting," she said.

He watched one tear roll down her cheek, a tiny Éarendel starship on its own journey. Why, he wondered, did he think he could save her from sorrow? Losses, old and new, plagued them both, and once again seemed close at hand. "I'm scheduled for training," he told her hoarsely — a newly commissioned soldier who, for now, had put poems, philology, and fantasy tales aside. "When I'm on leave," he said softly, "you and I will marry."

Chapter 6

THE WORLD HAD NEVER KNOWN such a war. Allied forces fought in territories stretching from Europe's Balkan Peninsula to South Africa, from Germany's Western Front in France and Belgium to the Pacific Ocean islands of Micronesia. Armies, equipped for the first time with machine guns and rapid-fire artillery, numbered not in the millions but in the tens of millions. By the end of this "War to End All Wars," in 1918, only two of Ronald's friends would still be alive.

Oxford graduates automatically received an officer's rank in the army, and Ronald was appointed second lieutenant. In August 1915, he was sent to training camp in Staffordshire. He was assigned to the Thirteenth Battalion of the Lancashire Fusiliers, not to the Nineteenth, where he might have fought alongside G. B. Smith. Trench drills and gun practice left him little spare time, but he managed to write a few letters and another poem.

Days, he wrote Edith, were gray and icy; he might spend the morning throwing small dummy bombs at targets, then burrow forward at lunchtime for a moment's warmth by an outdoor stove.

In early 1916, Ronald was transferred to the Eleventh Battalion of the Lancashire Fusiliers. England was cloaked in war: food was rationed; cities lay in nightly blackouts; households mourned dead husbands, brothers, and sons. When the French fortress of Verdun was attacked by Germans — suffering the heaviest artillery damage in history — Ronald knew his battalion would soon embark for France. Casualty lists from Verdun were so long that field officers didn't believe them. Hilary Tolkien, G. B. Smith, and R. Q. Gilson were in the army; Christopher Wiseman had joined the navy. Ronald sent all four men the poem he'd written at training camp, calling it "Kortirion among the Trees."

A short leave was granted, and deciding, after all, to seize the moment, Ronald took out a marriage license with Edith. Military pay, along with the small income kept for him by Father Francis, would cover Edith's living expenses — and after one of his poems, "Goblin Feet," was accepted for publication in *Oxford Poetry*, he and Edith considered their union blessed. On Wednesday, March 22, 1916, they wed in a Warwick church.

"I wish my parents could see us," Ronald told his new bride. "And if I'd had more leave, we could have gone to Birmingham and asked Father Francis to perform the ceremony."

Flushed with happiness, Edith nodded. "We outlasted his worry for us," she said. "Now that you're twenty-four and I'm twenty-seven, he might not even mention age!"

After a week's honeymoon outside Warwick, Ronald returned to his battalion, and Edith rented a village room near his camp. Wedded bliss, however, was soon met by harsher reality. The mail brought two notices: a group of Ronald's poems was rejected by publishers Sidgwick & Jackson, and embarkation to France was announced. Ronald would be sent to the French camp at Étaples, then to fields of German-manned trenches along the River Somme. British field marshals had scheduled a "Big Push," earmarking hundreds of thousands of Allied soldiers for a massive assault at the Somme. The plan, Ronald heard, was to break through German barbed wire, destroy the trenches, and gun down enemy troops.

Kissing Edith goodbye, he left for Étaples. En route, his sleeping bag, camp bed, mattress, and boots were stolen or lost. He borrowed what he could and, using some of his army pay, replaced the rest. After three weeks at the French camp, his battalion moved by train to the Somme and camped in a hamlet ten miles from the front line. Among fields of cornflowers and poppies were buildings blown apart by shells; in the distance was the constant crack of artillery fire.

On July 1, 1916, the Big Push began. Vast numbers of French and British soldiers pressed across muddy ground toward German barbed wire. All too quickly, they found themselves in trouble. The Allied Command, trying to provide enough supplies, had furnished each soldier with over sixty pounds of equipment. Moving under such weight was extremely slow and difficult; at the barbed wire, the men were easy targets for German guns.

When Ronald's battalion was ordered forward, the Battle of the Somme was already a disaster. Rain had turned the fields into mud baths. British tanks had either been destroyed by exploding shells or were stuck in the mud; soldiers, dead and wounded, their flesh torn, had fallen into bloody heaps. The first day's British casualties topped fifty thousand — with virtually no prisoners taken. Whole regiments were wiped out. Almost five months later, when the Battle of the Somme ended, casualties had reached the terrible sum of six hundred thousand for both Great Britain and Germany. Throughout Europe, almost a whole generation of young men was dead.

Ronald would never forget the horrors of war or the courage of the average soldier who fought beside him. He spent nearly three months at the Somme, crawling among corpses, the trees above him tilting like black skeletons, branches broken and shorn of leaves. After storming a huge fortification of German trenches, he cradled a dying soldier in his arms. Blood oozed over him and, in a moment of unusual silence, a field mouse darted across his fingers. With death and destruction around him, it seemed to Ronald that the mouse was a sole messenger of life.

In October, helping to dig mass graves, he contracted trench fever, a severe infection transmitted by ticks and lice. Thousands of other soldiers, wild-eyed from fever and rashes, were carried off the battlefield. Ronald was sent to a hospital at Le Touquet, where a despairing letter reached him from G. B. Smith. Their friend Rob Gilson, Smith wrote, had died at the front lines. Soon after reading the news, Ronald's temperature rose so high that he was shipped back to England and sent to a military hospital in Birmingham. There, Edith joined him. He spent many months in and out of the hospital, the infection waging its own war in his body. Never again would he be assigned to active duty.

At Christmas, a tragic note arrived from Christopher Wiseman. G. B. Smith had died from gangrene poisoning after being wounded in the right arm and thigh by a bursting shell. Ronald wondered if his friend had sensed that death was near. Only weeks earlier, he'd heard from him. "May God bless you, my dear John Ronald," Smith had written, "and may you say the things I have tried to say long after I am not there to say them, if such be my lot."

Christopher Wiseman and Ronald Tolkien were the only members of the T.C.B.S. to survive World War I. Lying in the hospital — G. B. Smith's words echoing in his mind — Ronald chose to take a great leap from his poetry. In the waning days of December, with dozens of his friends and acquaintances dead, he began a detailed history for his invented languages. What he crafted required an unprecedented act of artistry and mental power. Out of his own imagination, and with far more "sensible" tasks at hand, he would create an entire mythology.

The bleak morning light, leaving its pallor on the hospital cot, inched across his notebook. On the cover, in blue ink, he had printed *The Book of Lost Tales*. Inside he was writing what would become *The Silmarillion*, a volume of sagas. When Edith was not at his bedside, she spent hours neatly recopying various pages.

What he hoped, Ronald had told her, was to use his myths and legends as a foundation for the names, places, poetry, and songs in two of his languages — Quenya, based on Finnish, and a new language he'd invented, Sindarin, partially based on Welsh. When his head didn't throb from fever, he would say names aloud. "Gondolin, Beleriand, Doriath," he'd intone, names he gave to places. Carcharoth became his wolf; Morgoth, his Black Enemy; Olórin, his wisest angel.

Historically, myths were categorized by the cultures that spawned them: Greco-Roman, Judeo-Christian, Germanic, or Norse. After reading the thirteenth-century Norse myths in *The Elder Edda (or Poetic)* and *The Younger Edda (or Prose)*, or the German fables collected by the nineteenth-century Grimm brothers, or Longfellow's *Hiawatha*, Ronald regretted that England had no mythology. He wanted, therefore, to dedicate his tales "to England, to my country." Readers would be offered an explanation of his mythological world — its beginnings, its cycles, its creatures. This world would seem real to Ronald and, one day, to countless others, as if instead of inventing, he'd recorded "what was already 'there.'"

Dragons would be part of his mythology, as would great sword fights and wars. Sorrows and joys, chaos and cruelty would abound, but so would heroic goodness. He envisioned dark creatures named Balrogs and Orcs and gave new meaning to the word *elf*. In Ronald Tolkien's mythology, elves were not tiny sprites; they were men and women who never fell, as had humans, from God's grace. Elves were strong, artistic, intelligent, and brave. Unless slain in battle, they were immortal — unlike Ronald's mother and father.

The setting of *The Silmarillion*, our own planet in antiquity, was called Middle-earth — a Germanic expression for the world of humans. Creation came, explained Ronald, from the grace of Ilúvatar, the One, and through the music of his godly spirits. *The Silmarillion*'s longest story would involve three mystic jewels, the Silmarils, forged by Fëanor, greatest of elven craftsmen. The jewels were stolen by Morgoth, the Black Enemy; elves fought valiant wars to regain them. A shorter piece, which Ronald wrote for Edith, described the love of Beren, a mortal man, for Lúthien, an elf, whose father sets as her bride-price one of the stolen Silmarils. Beren and Lúthien's fate is "hopeless, yet not certain"; their devotion becomes their triumph.

In April of 1917, Ronald was released from the hospital. Assigned to inactive duty at a signaling camp in Yorkshire, he closed up his notebook. Yet in August, with the United States now fighting beside the Allies against the Central Powers, his fevers began again. Dizzy from head pain, he was admitted to Brooklands Officers'

Hospital in Hull, England. Edith packed up her belongings and moved nearby, but the daily trip to the hospital was tiring. Food was scarce and she was hungry. When she told Ronald she was pregnant, he insisted she limit her visits.

At Hull, Ronald continued *The Silmarillion*, writing of Túrin, the dragon slayer. He persuaded Edith to move back to Cheltenham with Jennie Grove until the baby was born. He, in turn, was feeling stronger. Reading to her from a page of his writing that she had copied, he said she must rest and enjoy nature. "Behold . . . ," he quoted, "the height and glory of the clouds, and the ever-changing mists; and listen to the fall of the rain upon the Earth!"

On November 16, 1917, Edith gave birth to a son. Ronald had been discharged from Brooklands and was back on duty at the Yorkshire camp. The message delivered to him, however, was grim; Edith's labor had been so difficult that her life was in danger. Distraught, Ronald felt the smothering ocean wave from his childhood nightmare. Yet by the time he was granted emergency leave and arrived, shaken, at the Cheltenham hospital, the crisis had miraculously passed. Though Edith was weakened, she had survived. Together, they named the baby John Francis Reuel Tolkien.

"*John* because of your first name," Edith whispered.

"Yes," Ronald said, tenderly wiping her forehead. "And *Francis* in honor of Father Francis."

"And *Reuel,*" Edith murmured before falling asleep, "in keeping with Tolkien tradition."

Picking up his son from a bassinet at the foot of Edith's bed, Ronald gazed at his small, perfect features. The baby, wrapped in a blue blanket, was suddenly precious to him — more precious than any of the three jewels, the Silmarils, could ever have been to Fëanor the elf. The beauty of the Silmarils, Ronald thought, contained the mystic light of creation. But the child in his arms, born on a cold day in Cheltenham during a fierce and terrible war, held the greater and brighter glory.

Chapter 7

MUSIC GRACED THE ROOMS OF the second-floor apartment on Oxford's St. John's Street. Ronald had paid movers to bring Edith's childhood piano from Birmingham storage into the apartment. She hadn't played for a long time, but now that the war had finally ended with an Allied victory and an armistice on November 11, 1918, she wanted to begin again. Hilary, one of the few young soldiers who'd survived and returned to England, came to visit baby John, talking of taking up apple farming in the Midlands, far from reminders of war. Since his own discharge, Ronald had worked part-time in Oxford for the *New English Dictionary* and tutored students in Anglo-Saxon. In the evenings, while Edith bathed John, Ronald wrote his *Silmarillion* mythology and invented another alphabet.

One evening, he anxiously listened to Edith play a Mozart sonata. "I have a chance," he said finally, "for a teaching post as Reader in English Language — at the University of Leeds."

Edith dropped her hands into her lap. "Oh . . . that's wonderful, Ronald. But Leeds is over one hundred fifty miles away."

"I'll find us a place there," he said, "if I'm the one chosen."

With his background and skills in philology, Ronald was offered the post. Accepting, he tried to ignore the sooty chimneys and gritty fog that marked the city of Leeds. When he learned that Edith was pregnant again, he rented a single room near the University; until the new baby was born, he would keep his family in Oxford and visit on weekends. On the train rides, he finished his latest tale, "The Fall of Gondolin," which he'd been told he could read to the Essay Club at Exeter College.

After Edith had given birth to Michael Hilary Reuel Tolkien in October 1920, the family lived in a small rented house in Leeds. Ronald took over the household chores and the care of little John. He tutored students and graded school examination papers for extra money, wrote poetry for literary magazines, and composed rhyming couplets for his mythology.

Seeking an academic life was, for Ronald, a way of staying close to the words that had soothed and entranced him since childhood. In his five years at Leeds, he would gain international recognition as a philologist and become the youngest professor on staff. His intense teaching style would influence the English department for years to come. Surrounded by books, libraries, and lecture halls, he could avoid the changes that dismayed him in the outside world: noisy motorcars now in mass production near Oxford; trees and meadows destroyed to make way for fuel stations and roads; pastoral towns, like his beloved Sarehole, swallowed up by growing cities.

In his office at the University of Leeds, beside gurgling water pipes, he prepared *A Middle English Vocabulary*, printed as a glossary in 1922. Collaborating with E. V. Gordon, an assistant lecturer at Leeds, he compiled the first edition of *Sir Gawain and the Green Knight* considered suitable for university study. Published in 1925, *Sir Gawain* was hailed as a major contribution to medieval literature and is used today in many colleges and universities.

Opening his lecture on *Beowulf*, Ronald would stride to the front of the room, look piercingly at his students — and then shout out a single word, *"HWAET!"* (Lo!), the start of this Old English poem. Like an actor, he'd breathe excitement into the word-by-word, verse-by-verse analysis that followed. During the school year, his students delighted in his Anglo-Saxon crossword puzzles or his abandoning his notes for a compelling, if unrelated, discussion topic. He helped pupils write and rewrite papers and books, often contributing the bulk of ideas but never allowing a credit line for himself.

In May of 1923, exhausted from preparing far more lectures than his contract required, Ronald developed pneumonia. He was juggling teaching duties, family life, and his writing. When he began to recover, he let Edith talk him into a holiday on the farm Hilary had bought in Evesham. "The children will love it," she'd told him. "You can teach them to climb trees."

In 1925, when he was only thirty-three years old, Ronald was offered a full professorship of Anglo-Saxon at Oxford University. He regretted leaving Leeds, but Oxford was irresistible to him. The house he rented on Oxford's Northmoor Road was just big enough for a third child — Christopher Reuel Tolkien — who had been born in November 1924 and named after Christopher Wiseman. The family moved again when a larger house became available next door. Two-storied, with a slate roof and surrounding tall trees, 20 Northmoor Road would shelter the Tolkiens for twenty-one years. In 1929, it welcomed a fourth and final child, Priscilla Mary Reuel Tolkien.

At Oxford, Ronald withdrew even further from what

he called the "horrors of twentieth-century progress." One weekend, he took Edith and the children to the outskirts of Birmingham. Among city streets, he found the rusted fence and gate that had led to the Sarehole cottage where he'd lived with his mother and Hilary. Now, cottage, willow trees, and the forbidden mushrooms were gone.

On a road with red signal lights and garbage cans, he came upon old Sarehole mill. No young boys stood gaping, as he and Hilary had done, for a glimpse of white bone dust or giant webs of leather belting. No waterwheel turned above a pit. "Look," he said to Edith. "My White Ogre and Black Ogre owned houses where that fuel station sits."

Edith touched his hand. He told her then about rolling pebbles down Sarehole's sandpit, about his mother's botany lessons in the flowery meadow, about the angry flash of Black Ogre's eyes. Wistfully, he gazed at his own children playing nearby; they were oblivious, of course, to all that once had been. "Only the landscape of love," Ronald said to his wife, memories sharp inside him, "will always endure."

"Chairs," or professorships, at Oxford were endowed by wealthy benefactors and given their names. Ronald held the chair of Rawlinson and Bosworth Professor of

Anglo-Saxon. He could now read, write, or speak Romance languages, Anglo-Saxon, Welsh, Icelandic, Finnish, German, Old German, Gothic, and other ancient tongues. His lecture schedule at Oxford was more hectic than it had been at Leeds. Required to present thirty-six lectures or classes per year, he scheduled 136. Still worrying over money, he kept tutoring pupils at home and grading papers. He'd also begun examiner work for other universities, sometimes traveling across England.

Weekday mornings he kissed Edith and the children goodbye, walked by the aviary at the side of the house so he could see the canaries, then bicycled to early Mass at St. Aloysius Catholic Church. Afterward, if the clock at Merton College hadn't yet struck 8:30, he might stop at the Covered Market to buy sausages for Edith. In his bicycle basket were his Oxford gown, briefcase, and pipe. "In spite of the motorcars," he'd say, "bicycles are in charge on all the narrow streets."

Most of Ronald's lectures were in the Examination Schools building. Students found him brilliant and warmhearted, though some had difficulty following his quick, run-on speech. He often lectured as if in conversation with himself, presuming he'd be understood. Throughout the English Department, his impact was enormous. He convinced a skeptical administration to change the curriculum, adding a course in Icelandic and requiring, in the study of philology, the actual *reading* of early and medieval literature. He suggested measures for healing an old rift between "Lang" and "Lit," the language and literature divisions, and he inspired many students to make a career of what they'd previously considered a dry subject — philology.

To most observers, Ronald was the consummate scholar. Even students who saw his whimsical side had no notion of his love for dragons, goblins, and gremlins — or the immortal elves who filled *The Silmarillion*. He wrote the book mostly in secret, a task that kept him awake at night. His mythology was so detailed that he wanted every piece of it to fit the whole. He knew other scholars might laugh at his "fairy-tale fantasies," but he saw them as something more — as a reason for his invented languages and a means of modernizing myths so they could give strength, comfort, and even hope in a frequently harsh and dangerous world.

If his children wanted a bedtime story, he created that, too. When John couldn't sleep, he was told of Carrots, the red-haired boy who climbed into a cuckoo clock and had odd adventures. When Michael awoke from nightmares, he heard about Rover, the dog turned into a toy by a mean wizard. John and Michael liked their father's tales as much as playing with model trains. And not only the children enjoyed the stories. Edith, who'd been happiest in Leeds, was shy and awkward among the sophisticated wives of Oxford professors. She suffered from headaches and would ask Ronald to sit with her. "Tell me a story," she'd say. "Tell me of Barrow-wight the ghost, or Chrysophylax the dragon."

It was during the 1930s that Ronald completed new academic works. His papers on variations of fourteenth-century English in Chaucer's *Reeve's Tale* and on language history in the *Ancrene Wisse*, a medieval instruction book for religious recluses, met with praise. In 1936, he presented a lecture, "*Beowulf*: The Monsters and the Critics," to the British Academy. *Beowulf*, he said, was a vital, heroic poem, not a dry literary corpse to be autopsied; its monsters and dragon should not be taken lightly. "A dragon is no idle fancy," he explained. "Even today (despite the critics), you may find men . . . caught by the fascination of the worm." The following year, "*Beowulf*: The Monsters and the Critics" was published and gained wide recognition as a masterpiece of literary criticism.

One summer day, Ronald sat in his study on Northmoor Road grading exam papers. His desk faced a window overlooking the trees and flowers in a neighbor's garden. Behind him were bookcases and a table filled with notes on a translation he'd made of *Pearl*, a Middle English poem about a dead child. Topping the notes, like a colorful toy, was an illustrated copy of *Jack and the Beanstalk*, the only fairy tale he'd found in all his research that was native to England.

Holding his pen over an examination page, Ronald read through several paragraphs of scribbled writing. Had his mother been alive, he told himself, she'd have questioned the student's faulty penmanship. Turning the page, he was surprised to find it blank, probably by mistake. Gratefully, he considered the clean whiteness of the paper. Nothing to judge, nothing to correct. He glanced up toward the window, watching the waving leaves of a sycamore tree. In *The Silmarillion*, two trees from the earliest age of Middle-earth — reminiscent of sun and moon — had been the source of the radiant light of the Silmarils.

Suddenly, without a plan, Ronald pressed his pen onto the blank examination page and wrote out a sentence: "In a hole in the ground," he wrote, "there lived a hobbit." Staring at his words, he searched for meaning or a clue. *What*, he asked himself, *is a hobbit? What did it look like? What did it do? Why did it live in a hole in the earth?*

Little did Ronald know that he was about to embark

on a journey that would jolt him out of his academic life, keeping him on Middle-earth, where hobbits lived, as often as in the city of Oxford, England. Ronald would set out on a quest: this time to discover "what hobbits were like." The answers he found would bring him a fame he had never sought.

Chapter 8

AFTER THE EVENING COALS WERE snuffed out and Edith and the children were asleep, Ronald would climb the stairs to the attic. He'd sit on a camp bed, writing in his latest notebook. A keyhole desk was stuffed with papers and an old Hammond typewriter. It didn't matter that the next day would be crowded with lectures, that the Coalbiters — a group Ronald had formed to read Icelandic literature — would convene at the Edgewood Hotel, or that he had supper plans with his friend, fellow writer and lecturer C. S. Lewis. Nor did it matter that thirteen-year-old John needed to be fetched from boarding school in Berkshire or that Ronald had promised to plant tomato seeds with six-year-old Christopher; he put off sleeping to spend several hours alone in the attic, "discovering" a hobbit named Bilbo Baggins.

Hobbits, he wrote, were little folks "half our height," living in elaborate underground holes in the Shire region of Middle-earth. They wore no shoes because their feet grew "natural leathery soles and thick warm brown hair." Fond of colorful clothes, gardens, food, and tobacco ("pipe weed"), they were good-natured but shy. Bilbo, an ordinary hobbit, never did anything rash or unexpected. One day, however, while having tea, he was visited by thirteen dwarves and the Wizard Gandalf. Against all his objections (*We don't want any adventures here, thank you!*), he was whisked off with his visitors on a risky mission: retrieving treasure stolen from the dwarves by the ferocious dragon Smaug.

Ronald's hobbit story grew into a children's novel. He finished a handwritten draft in the early 1930s, passing it around "for fun" among several friends and students. He was busy with a coveted philology grant he'd won in 1934, based partially on his paper on the *Ancrene Wisse*, which had broken new academic ground. He'd shown that passages in that book were not just rough West Midland dialect, but a polished language that could be traced to pre-Conquest times. How could an Oxford professor, most of Ronald's colleagues would later agree, be hailed for his scholarship, be considered one of the world's foremost philologists, and even *think* of writing a *fairy tale*?

The Hobbit, as Ronald's book came to be called, contained the wonder of fantasy along with deep morality and wisdom. Good and evil battle across the pages as Bilbo Baggins learns he is capable of adventures. To Ronald, even the most ordinary person — or hobbit — could turn out to have heroic possibilities. Bilbo, no longer a passive, self-satisfied "homebody," becomes a little warrior, taking responsibility for himself and others. Almost killed by goblins and giant spiders, nearly eaten by trolls and a spooky creature named Gollum, he finally confronts the fiery dragon Smaug in a mountain tunnel. ("Going on from there," Ronald wrote of Bilbo, "was the bravest thing he ever did.") Caught in a Battle of Five Armies (dwarves, elves, men, goblins, and wild wolves), Bilbo finally triumphs on behalf of justice. He may not be a hero who creates magic or kills dragons — but he has, Ronald would explain, "the indomitable [and heroic] courage of quite small people against impossible odds."

For Ronald, the Shire countryside of the hobbits represented everything he loved about England's West Midlands — Worcestershire, where his mother's family, the Suffields, had lived, and, of course, Sarehole. He named Bilbo Baggins's home Bag-End, a nickname given by Worcestershire neighbors to his aunt Jane's farm. He likened himself to Bilbo. "I am, in fact, a hobbit," he'd write, "in all but size. I like gardens, trees, and unmechanized farmlands; I smoke a pipe, and like good plain food. . . . I do not travel much."

Pieces of Old Norse and Icelandic myths appear in *The Hobbit*. Names of dwarves — Durin, Thorin, Gloin, Bifur, Bofur, Fili, and Kili — were borrowed from *The Elder Edda;* Mirkwood Forest, where Bilbo and his companions suffer various terrors, is found in an Icelandic saga; and a deadly riddle game between Bilbo and Gollum, the hissing creature who speaks of himself as "my preciouss-ss-ss," also has roots in ancient mythology. Binding both past and present in *The Hobbit* is Ronald's great love of language, evident in the riddles and songs:

Song:
The dwarves of yore made mighty spells,
While hammers fell like ringing bells
In places deep, where dark things sleep,
In hollow halls beneath the fells. . . .

RIDDLE:
This thing all things devours:
Birds, beasts, trees, flowers;
Gnaws iron, bites steel;
Grinds hard stones to meal;

Slays kings, ruins town,
And beats high mountain down.
(ANSWER: *Time*)

Only because an editor at London's George Allen &
Unwin Publishers heard about *The Hobbit* and asked to
see it was the book published. In order to quickly submit
a typed copy of the handwritten manuscript, Ronald
had been typing well past midnight; then sixteen-year-
old Michael Tolkien, who'd cut his right hand on a
school window, insisted on helping his father by pounding away on the typewriter with his left hand. When the
manuscript arrived at Allen & Unwin, chairman Stanley
Unwin paid his ten-year-old son, Rayner, a shilling for a
child's view of the book. Rayner was excited over *The
Hobbit*, talking of Bilbo's grand adventure "fighting goblins and wargs" and of the "terrific battle" with Smaug
the dragon.

With a map and illustrations drawn by Ronald himself, *The Hobbit* was published in England in 1937. To
Ronald's amazement, the London *Times* praised it:

All who love that kind of children's book
which can be read and re-read by adults
should note that a new star has appeared
in this constellation. . . . The truth is that

in this book a number of good things, never before united, have come together: a fund of humor, an understanding of children, and a happy fusion of the scholar's with the poet's grasp of mythology. On the edge of a valley one of Professor Tolkien's characters can pause and say: "It smells like elves." It may be years before we produce another author with such a nose for an elf. The professor has an air of inventing nothing. He has studied trolls and dragons at first hand and describes them with . . . fidelity . . .

Ronald's former student, W. H. Auden, a renowned poet, called *The Hobbit* "the best children's story written in the last fifty years." Slowly, the book turned up on bookshelves in schools, libraries, and homes. Though some of Ronald's colleagues denounced what they called "his foolishness" and condemned him for "slumming," *The Hobbit* was the talk of England. Admiring neighbor children would stop Ronald on the street to ask about Bilbo. "He has written down his adventures," Ronald would tell boys and girls. "He mentions them in *The Hobbit — There and Back Again, a Hobbit's Holiday*."

In 1938, *The Hobbit* was published in the United States by Houghton Mifflin Company. At year's end, it had won the New York *Herald Tribune's* prize for Best Children's Book of 1938. No one was more astonished than Ronald that the little hobbit named Bilbo Baggins, first discovered by him, unlikely though it seemed, while he graded exam papers, and who was a "kindly little soul" with "brave heart" and "woolly toes," was becoming a household name.

His days were crowded before, and now the pace quickened. No sooner did *The Hobbit* show success than Stanley Unwin asked Ronald to write another hobbit story. Thinking Bilbo was living happily "to the end of his days" in the Shire, Ronald was more interested in offering Allen & Unwin his latest draft of *The Silmarillion*. But Stanley Unwin, though fascinated by the mythology, did not want to publish it. He had struck pay dirt with *The Hobbit*; he requested a sequel.

Ronald considered a tale about a hobbit named Bingo. Yet his nights were spent disliking the idea. Mostly, he wanted to sit in his son Christopher's room, watching the boy sleep. Only months before, Christopher was diagnosed as having heart problems and had since left school to rest in bed. Ronald spent hours with the boy, telling him stories that did not need to be typed up and sent away. Though Edith worried over Christopher, it was Ronald who was depressed. The success of *The Hobbit* suddenly seemed unimportant to him.

Dragons of loss were spitting fire again; they loomed above him, untamed.

"Come to bed," a sleepy Edith would tell him, standing in her nightdress in Christopher's doorway. "Tomorrow, a graduate student comes for tutoring and you have lectures at Balliol College. C. S. Lewis's literary club, the Inklings, will meet. You'll be tired if you don't sleep."

"I think Christopher is stronger," Ronald might answer. "Perhaps his heart isn't fragile. There's a rosy color in his cheeks."

As Christopher's health improved, Ronald finally began what he called "the new *Hobbit*." Though his son's illness had deeply wearied him, he felt pulled to keep at his writing, hoping he'd find a good story line between words he'd crossed out or revised. Even when colleagues still criticized *The Hobbit*, dismissing its success, Ronald believed that his published children's book pivoted on the same classic structure — a mythic journey or quest — found in ancient sagas. He wanted to carry that structure into his new book.

In 1939, Ronald accepted an invitation to give the Andrew Lang Lecture at Scotland's University of St. Andrew. While he only liked traveling to the countryside, he made this trip to the city because it was Andrew Lang's fairy tales that he'd read as a child. His lecture, "On Fairy-Stories," analyzed the function of fairy tale and myth. Eight years later, recognized as a vital contribution to literature, it was published by the Oxford University Press.

Fairy tales, Ronald said, are not just for children. Often not "stories about fairies" at all, they tell of adventures in the "Perilous Realm." Like myths, they provide a vision of life as it ought to be — where good ultimately wins over evil. People in pain or sorrow may find more comfort in fairy-tale dragons, goblins, heroes, and magic than in real life. Fantasy, as Ronald explained, brings people the "recovery" of seeing things differently, the "escape" from human limitations, and the "consolation" of a happy ending.

To write fairy tales, Ronald said, one must be a "sub-creator" of a "Secondary World" that the mind enters. Then, "what . . . [the writer] relates is 'true': it accords with the laws of that world. You therefore believe it, while you are, as it were, inside." If a fantasy world is consistent enough with the real world — even though it may contain "impossible" elements like talking trees — it feels comfortable. The sub-creator hasn't ignored reality but is keenly aware of it, building a Secondary World that already seems to exist.

Ronald stopped revising *The Silmarillion* to plunge into the Secondary World of his sequel for Stanley Unwin. In *The Hobbit*, when Bilbo had come upon slimy

Gollum, he'd found and kept a magic ring that made the wearer invisible. On a notebook page, Ronald wrote: "Make *return of ring* a motive . . . it exacts its penalty. You must either lose it, or *yourself*." In the attic at Northmoor Road, Ronald met some chilling characters who searched for Bilbo and the ring. Sometimes they seemed to appear out of the night, like the Black Riders or Ring-wraiths, who were permanently invisible beneath their clothes and hideously cruel.

What is the source of the magic ring? Ronald wondered. *What are its powers? Is it good or evil? Had it truly belonged to Gollum?* On a family holiday at Sidmouth resort, he shared these questions with Edith and the children. His family, intrigued by the story, was well and happy. Christopher's heart was normal; John was teaching at Exeter College; Michael studied at Trinity; Priscilla, sweet and gracious, was only ten years old. Perhaps it was knowing that the dragons had, for now, left his family alone that gave Ronald the answers to the haunting but sinister ring.

Hiking across the red, circular hills at Sidmouth, he found that the ring was the One Ruling Ring of twenty rings. It was sought by an evil power, Sauron, from Middle-earth's dark land of Mordor. Gollum had stolen the One Ring; Bilbo had found it by accident; now Sauron wanted it back in order to rule and destroy the world. Hope, Ronald knew, lay in someone brave and good — a hobbit, perhaps — carrying the Ring (at great risk and for hundreds of miles) to Mordor and casting it into the fires in one of the "Cracks of Doom."

The "new *Hobbit*" did not feel like a children's book to Ronald. It was deeper, more frightening. It might prove unsuitable for Allen & Unwin and lie in the attic alongside *The Silmarillion* — but it had suddenly come alive. When Ronald returned to his teaching duties, he wrote a letter to Stanley Unwin. The new book, he said, was moving with Bilbo, Gandalf, Gollum, and another hobbit, Frodo, toward "unforeseen goals," yet its Secondary World was in place. Out of the depths of myth, fairy tale, and Middle-earth, the book had already named itself. It was called *The Lord of the Rings*.

Chapter 9

Three Rings for the Elven-kings under the sky,
Seven for the Dwarf-lords in their halls of stone,
Nine for Mortal Men doomed to die,
One for the Dark Lord on his dark throne
In the Land of Mordor where the Shadows lie.
One Ring to rule them all, One Ring to find them,
One Ring to bring them all and in the darkness bind them
In the Land of Mordor where the Shadows lie.
(OPENING POEM, THE LORD OF THE RINGS, THE TWO TOWERS)

Ronald was suddenly a traveler, though mostly on private journeys. After lecturing at Pembroke, Balliol, or Merton, after stoking the coals in his study or cleaning his pipe, he would "board" Éarendel's starship, destined for Middle-earth. *The Hobbit* had been a pleasure to write, a bedtime tale for his children. *The Lord of the Rings* was not the same. It pulled at him, a dizzying storm. Trying to make chapter outlines, he had to throw them away. The characters had taken over, living their own stories, leaving him control over only his invented languages. Though he'd created "elf song" in *The Hobbit*, he would go further this time, depicting various cultures and peoples by how they spoke — the true ground of philology.

Elves, the immortal race, spoke his most noble languages, Quenya and Sindarin. Dwarves, trolls, Orcs, hobbits, and others had their own speech or dialect. On Middle-earth, language could soothe or stab, be exalted or weak, sound coarse and common or ripe and brave. When Sauron had forged the One Ruling Ring, he'd also bred Orcs to guard over it. "Filled with malice, hating even their own kind," Orcs spoke the harsh, guttural Black Speech of Sauron, pronouncing words at the back of the throat ("Uruk-hai"), in contrast to the silken sounds of elf language ("Lothlórien" or "Elendil").

Ronald's new book would contain great battles and bloodshed as the good on Middle-earth fought against the evil. Back on earth itself, other battles brewed that would lead, in 1939, to World War II. Many future readers of *The Lord of the Rings* compared Sauron to Germany's Adolf Hitler, but Ronald insisted that he'd meant no link. What he did mean to show was his concern for the environment and his aching regret over "progress" ravaging the land. Long before environmentalism was a cause, he'd been a believer. Amid the suspense, glory, and terror in his book were beautifully crafted descriptions of nature — mountains, prairies, and forests; sunlight, starlight, wind, rain, and snow. As Frodo left the elven land of Lórien by boat, Ronald wrote:

> The breeze died away and the River flowed without a sound. No voice of bird broke the silence. The sun grew misty as the day grew old, until it gleamed in a pale sky like a high white pearl. Then it faded into the West, and dusk came early, followed by a grey and starless night. . . . Great trees passed by like ghosts, thrusting their twisted thirsty roots through the mist down into the water. . . . Frodo sat and listened to the faint lap and gurgle of the River fretting among the tree-roots and driftwood near the shore, until his head nodded and he fell into an uneasy sleep.

During World War II, Ronald was divided even more between Middle-earth and home. While Frodo carried the burden of Sauron's Ring, two Tolkien sons carried the burdens of war. John, who had trained for the priesthood in Rome, was evacuated to Lancashire, and Michael was an antiaircraft gunner. Though Oxford was never bombed, food was scarce, especially meat and sugar, and Ronald brought hens into the garden to provide eggs. He became an air-raid warden, stationed on certain nights in a clammy hut that served as a local headquarters for surveillance. As he worried over his sons, he kept juggling his writing with his teaching. Paragraphs ran onto thousands of scraps of paper. Developing stomach ulcers, he drank rationed milk that Edith warmed for him, but she was ill herself with arthritis and migraine headaches. "At fifty and forty-seven," she told him, "we're not the spring chickens in the garden."

By 1940, Ronald was editing texts of Nordic and Anglo-Saxon literature for the Oxford University Press, coediting the Oxford English Monograph Series, and writing a short tale, *Farmer Giles of Ham*. He was also deep into a crisis in *The Lord of the Rings*. Frodo, as unlikely a hero as Bilbo, had taken on the "doomed" mission of destroying the Ring and saving the peoples of Middle-earth. "Yet such is oft the course," Ronald wrote, "of deeds that move the wheels of the world; small hands do them because they must, while the eyes of the great are elsewhere."

Frodo is accompanied on his mission by the Fellowship of the Ring: Legolas (an elf); Sam, Merry, and Pippin (hobbits); Gimli (a dwarf); Gandalf (the Wizard); Boromir (a man); and Aragorn (a man also known as the mysterious Strider). On the way to Mordor, Frodo is stabbed by a sneering Black Rider (or Nazgûl) but miraculously survives. He meets ghastly monsters and creatures — and witnesses, in the underground Mines of Moria, the devastating death of Gandalf. His two friends, Merry and Pippin, are captured by Orcs, but while Aragorn, Legolas, and Gimli try to rescue them, Frodo continues his deadly journey with his closest friend, Sam.

Urged by his children, Ronald added several characters to *The Lord of the Rings*. "Papa, can you name someone in your book after my favorite doll?" Priscilla asked him. And so was born Tom Bombadil, a man of spiritual power. "I love trees, Papa, as much as you do," Michael said. "Can trees who talk appear in the book?" Thus came the fourteen-foot-tall Ents, oldest of all races on Middle-earth, guardians of Fangorn Forest. Treebeard, the eldest Ent, made funny noises when he spoke (*"Hrum, hoom"*) as did Ronald's friend C. S. Lewis.

Gollum became a main character in the book. Having once stolen the Ring, he was maimed by its power. Crafty and repulsive, obsessed with finding the Ring after losing it to Bilbo, who'd "put his hand on it, blindly, in the dark," Gollum follows Frodo to Mordor. ("The thing was eating up his mind, of course," said Gandalf of Gollum, "and the torment [was] almost unbearable.")

As Ronald told the story that he wanted readers to accept as "actual history," the Ring became, for him, a symbol of the danger in letting oneself be possessed by power or evil ("The very desire of it corrupts the heart"). Sauron, the ultimate evil in *The Lord of the Rings*, has only one eye — but the eye has no lid, because Sauron never sleeps. Whatever is good, Ronald would say as he traveled between his two worlds, must be preserved and protected with all one's strength, heart, and wits — even if other Saurons might lie ahead.

Some of Ronald's colleagues talked about him behind his back. *Professor Tolkien, they said, has already compromised his scholarship by writing that lowly fairy tale,* The Hobbit. *Worse, it's popular enough to let everyone know how far he's stooped. It may have garnered some . . . ah . . . impressive reviews, but the reviewers weren't of Oxford's ilk. Besides, Tolkien isn't meeting his obligations. Where is his introduction to the new* Beowulf *translation? He has time to read his latest mush to that Inklings club, but not enough time to translate* Pearl *from Middle English.* ("*Hrum, hoom,*" Treebeard the Ent might have said.)

It was true that Ronald had been spending more

hours on Middle-earth than at home. He just couldn't bear leaving Frodo in peril. Merry and Pippin are rescued, Gandalf arises from the dead, and Aragorn turns out to be the lost king of the kingdom of Gondor, now under siege by Sauron. Near Mordor, Frodo and Sam are tracked by the dreadful Gollum. They force him to lead them on a route less guarded by Sauron's henchmen; little do they know he is delivering them into the poisonous clutches of the spider Shelob:

> All living things were her food, and her vomit darkness. . . . [She was] horrible beyond the horror of an evil dream. Most like a spider she was, but huger than the great hunting beasts. . . . Great horns she had, and behind her short stalk-like neck was her huge swollen body, a vast bloated bag, swaying and sagging between her legs; its great bulk was black, blotched with livid marks, but the belly underneath was pale and luminous and gave forth a stench. Her legs were bent, with great knobbed joints high above her back, and hair that stuck out like steel spines, and at each leg's end there was a claw.

Shelob reminded Ronald of his childhood scare with the tarantula, when his nurse had sucked the venom from his foot. Middle-earth itself called to days of the past. Though its mythology told of darkness and evil spirits, it also sang of a golden age of heroes and glory—a stark contrast to twentieth-century war, hunger, and cruelty. Evil, Ronald believed, could never be totally erased, but it could wither and fail against strength and imagination.

At times, Ronald thought he was failing at *The Lord of the Rings*. The story was far from finished—years were passing as it unraveled. During dry periods, he could not write a word. He might lose Frodo and Sam, or see the glint of Aragorn's mighty sword without knowing where it would strike, or wish only to rest against Treebeard's gnarled trunk. For one whole year, instead of writing, he scrupulously drew maps of Middle-earth's terrain, attending to every detail of routes taken by the Fellowship of the Ring. He made certain that time and distance were figured perfectly; he charted phases of the moon and the direction of the wind. Geography, chronology (of the various cycles of Middle-earth), and calendars consumed entire notebooks. Watercolor sketches hung on the walls. Since the Fellowship moved mainly on foot, he used a British Army survey to determine exactly how far soldiers could travel on marches.

"If you say aloud names from your book," Edith told him, "you'll put aside your maps and write again. I know how you love the names, Ronald."

"Yes," he agreed, reaching again into the past. "Nantyglo and Senghenydd," he said, remembering the coal trucks. "My mother would find me at the window, practicing those names." He stood by the fireplace in his study, waving his pipe in the air. "Faramir, son of Denethor," he pronounced in a booming voice, naming a hero from *The Lord of the Rings*. "Arwen, daughter of Elrond. Théoden; Galadriel."

Soon he was writing of the battle between Sauron's dark forces and the people of Gondor. Bloodier than the fight at Helm's Deep, where Aragorn, Legolas, and Gimli had fought Orcs and Wolf-riders, Gondor's war brought the Black Riders. ("Ever they circled above the City, like vultures that expect their fill of doomed men's flesh.") Orcs constructed huge catapults that hurled flaming "missiles" upon Minas Tirith, Gondor's chief city. The missiles, however, were actually the heads of those who had fallen fighting in defense of Gondor:

> They were grim to look on; for though
> some [heads] were crushed and shapeless,
> and some had been cruelly hewn, yet many
> had features that could be told, and it

seemed that they had died in pain; and all were branded with the foul token of the Lidless Eye.

As Ronald wrote of war, his villains remained unmerciful; his heroes, however, persevered even when hope was gone. The war from Mordor merged for him with the tragedy of World War II's Holocaust. By 1944, his son Christopher was trained as a pilot, Sauron and Hitler both wielded their evils, and the worlds of past and present seemed in disarray.

Writing and revising, Ronald kept Christopher abreast of the book through letters. Sometimes he became overwhelmed by the feeling that, unlike his heroes, he might *not* go on. Papers filled his study in bulging boxes and drawers. Yet he rallied enough in those months to keep himself going. He told his son, "It is no good growing faint." And at Oxford, to the chagrin of colleagues who still demeaned him, he was appointed to the distinguished chair of Merton Professor of English Language and Literature.

At the end of World War II, Ronald moved Edith, Priscilla, and himself to a smaller house. Christopher came home to visit, John was a priest in the Midlands, and Michael, married and teaching school, had an infant son. By December 1947, ten and a half years after starting *The Lord of the Rings*, Ronald completed a massive first draft. He was fifty-five years old. He continued to revise the manuscript until late 1949, refining the idea that evil can be an unknowing instrument for good. On Mount Doom, the Ring has finally overtaken long-suffering but loyal Frodo — who bears it on a finger. Gollum bites off Frodo's finger, snatches the Ring ("my preciouss-ss-ss!"), then accidentally topples with it into the fires. With Gollum's act, the Fellowship of the Ring and Frodo's mission have triumphed. The Ring is destroyed, Sauron is thrust from his evil throne, and Middle-earth is saved:

> There rose a huge shape of shadow [Sauron], impenetrable, lightning-crowned, filling all the sky. Enormous it reared above the world, and stretched out towards them a vast threatening hand, terrible but impotent; for even as it leaned over them, a great wind took it, and it was all blown away, and passed; and then a hush fell.

Ronald wept as he finished the book. He had lived on Middle-earth so long, he didn't know how to leave it. Nor did he know if he had created an unwieldy monster or a readable tale. *The Hobbit* still sold briskly, bringing royalty checks and praise from readers, but the mythology of *The Lord of the Rings* might prove too dense. With his bulky manuscript wrapped in paper, he penned a note to Stanley Unwin: "It is written," he said of the book, "in my life-blood, such as that is, thick or thin; and I can no other."

The Lord of the Rings arrived in 1950 at the offices of Allen & Unwin. Since Rayner Unwin, who now worked for his father, was away on business, an editor unfamiliar with Ronald's work read the book. Several weeks later, a package arrived at the Tolkien home. Opening it, Ronald could feel the weight of judgment under his fingers. Quickly, manuscript pages tumbling from him, he skimmed the cover note. *The Lord of the Rings*, said the note, was rejected. The editor was not suggesting revisions. He did not ask to see the book again.

"Take heart," Frodo whispered to Ronald from Middle-earth. "Don't ever leave us."

Chapter 10

FOR MONTHS, RONALD RETREATED, OFTEN sitting in his study beside an ash-filled stove, lost in thought, missing his home on Middle-earth. At night, he dreamed he was in Mordor's desolate Dead Marshes, where thousands of men and elves had perished in battle. Frodo, Sam, and Gollum had found the marshes; in swampy pools were phantom faces of dead warriors. Ronald felt himself being pulled down among the dead. Some nights, he caught a glimpse of his mother or father. Once, he saw Father Francis's stern face and the haunted eyes of his T.C.B.S. friends, G. B. Smith and Rob Gilson.

Edith finally persuaded him to try another publisher for *The Lord of the Rings*. Reluctantly, he sent the manuscript to London's William Collins and Sons; they replied that to publish the book, they'd have to cut it in half. Another publisher remarked, "Unsalable." But when Rayner Unwin discovered what had happened in his absence, he asked to see the book. Wary of a second rejection from Allen & Unwin, Ronald dragged his feet and only mailed the manuscript after weeks of saying "No."

Rayner Unwin cabled his father, who was in Japan, that *The Lord of the Rings*, while extremely long, was a "work of genius." The cost of paper, ink, typesetting, and binding would be high, and the book would probably lose £1,000 ($2,800), but the initial investment could be reduced by printing it in three volumes over three years. "If you think it a work of genius," said a return cable from Stanley Unwin to his son, "then you may lose £1,000."

Ronald balked at having his book split into three parts, but wanted it published. Though he knew readers might laugh at his "grown-up *Hobbit*," he felt it could be useful in the world. If he'd succeeded at showing the power of language and myth; if he'd made it clear that good could win over evil, but that its victory must be earned anew by each individual; if he'd proven that land needed protection and that Mordor might exist anywhere, then he had contributed something of worth.

He planned appendices for *The Lord of the Rings*, wanting to further explain the 37,063 years of Middle-earth — its kingdoms and people, its languages, nomenclatures, calendars, wars, climates, agriculture, and geography. He chose titles for his three volumes: *The Fellowship of the Ring, The Two Towers,* and *The Return of the King.* He was late finishing his appendices, and Allen & Unwin had to order special typesetting keys for the strange shapes of the Elvish script, but when they arrived, the manuscript was complete. In 1954, *The Fellowship of the Ring* rolled off the presses.

Then came the waiting. Ronald was the "defendant in court" who had argued his own case; critics, after deliberation, would return their verdicts. For the first time in months, Ronald slept soundly. He had done all he could; he'd written "his heart out," he said, and he felt as Sam had during an attack by Orcs — "For a moment, his own fate . . . ceased to trouble him."

When early reviews arrived, Ronald read them with Edith, helping her arthritic fingers hold the paper. Eighteen years had passed since he'd begun *The Lord of the Rings.* At age sixty-two, an elder scholar at Oxford, he had traveled far on Middle-earth. He'd wandered a lush ground of mythology, slaying his dragons and demons — believing that truth and courage could survive.

"Here are beauties," said C. S. Lewis's review of *The Fellowship of the Ring,* "which pierce like swords or burn like cold iron; here is a book that will break your heart . . . good beyond hope." "The severely practical," said an Oxford *Times* review, "will have no time for it. Those who have imagination to kindle will find themselves completely carried along, becoming part of the eventful quest." Some reviewers criticized the book's prose style; others found the plot "silly." But sales, while small, were steadier than Allen & Unwin had predicted. The book moved by "word of mouth"; republished by Houghton Mifflin Company in the United States, it swept among U.S. college students, often disappearing permanently from library shelves. By the time the second volume of *The Lord of the Rings* was issued the following year, readers were demanding the third.

In academic circles, Ronald remained a curiosity. He'd been awarded honorary Doctor of Letters degrees by both University College in Dublin, Ireland, and University of Liège in Belgium. He'd presented the William Paton Ker Memorial Lecture in Glasgow, Scotland, and was elected vice president of the Philological Society of Great Britain. Yet, amid academic papers, reference books, and texts translated or written by him were his fanciful stories of Ents and Orcs, Balrogs and Barrowwights.

In the fall of 1955, ahead of schedule, the final volume of Ronald's book was published. Clamoring buyers lined up at London bookstores, asking for "that tale by the Oxford professor." Shop owners stocked all three volumes at the cashier's counter. Before long, Allen &

Unwin announced that the first edition of *The Lord of the Rings* had sold out, making it a collector's item. Rayner Unwin's concern over losing £1,000 evaporated; according to the order sheets, J.R.R. Tolkien's sequel to *The Hobbit* was outselling other titles on the market. When Ronald appeared at a monthly meeting of the Inklings, he was given a standing ovation.

Reviews now appeared in magazines, journals, and newspapers that had waited to comment on *The Lord of the Rings* until all three volumes were available. "An extraordinary, a distinguished piece of work," said New York's *Herald Tribune*. "One of the best wonder-tales ever written," gushed Boston's *Herald Traveler*. A dissenting voice, however, was American literary critic Edmund Wilson. In his review, "Oo, Those Awful Orcs!," Wilson called *The Lord of the Rings* "a children's book, which has somehow gotten out of hand. . . . What we get is a simple confrontation — in more or less the traditional terms of British melodrama — of the forces of Evil with the forces of Good, the remote and alien villain with the plucky little homegrown hero. . . . Dr. Tolkien has little skill at narrative and no instinct for literary form."

Children, to the surprise of both Edmund Wilson and publishing pundits, joined the readership of *The Lord of the Rings*. Many children managed to tackle the immense, three-volume story, fascinated by its characters. In September 1955, the British Broadcasting Corporation (BBC) serialized the book on radio, broadcasting it in ten parts to nearly twenty-eight thousand schools and more than five million young people.

If, as critic Edmund Wilson had claimed, *The Lord of the Rings* was a children's book that had "somehow gotten out of hand," millions of adults in a growing number of countries vehemently disagreed. Sales of the three volumes prompted new printings by Allen & Unwin. Bookstores, schools, and libraries kept ordering copies. Not only were readers making J.R.R. Tolkien, philology scholar, a continued commercial success, they were turning him into a hero.

FRODO LIVES!

GANDALF FOR PRESIDENT!

J.R.R. TOLKIEN IS HOBBIT-FORMING!

By the mid-1960s, Tolkien mottoes appeared on lapel buttons and subway walls in the United States. *The Lord of the Rings* was one of the most popular works of fiction in American publishing. Campus stores at Harvard and Yale couldn't keep the book in stock. Students, facing society with its growing materialism, violence, and greed, were looking for "a better way" to act as adults.

Many joined the Peace Corps or VISTA; many fought for civil rights, disarmament, or environmental protection. Stunned by the 1963 assassination of President John F. Kennedy and the 1965 landing of U.S. Marines in Vietnam, they embraced *The Lord of the Rings*. It spoke to them of virtues of the past and a love of life and land; it gave them a new mythology.

Middle-earth appealed to readers. Ronald had compiled so many details and descriptions, all woven together into his Secondary World, that the story of Middle-earth lingered on the edge of reality. "One of the most remarkable works of literature," said Bernard Levin in the journal *Truth*, "in our, or any, time."

In June of 1965, an unauthorized U.S. paperback of *The Lord of the Rings* was issued by Ace Books. Houghton Mifflin rushed to put out an authorized version, hoping Ronald would make immediate revisions to fit the copyright laws. As usual, he was late on delivery. He'd written a novella, *Smith of Wootton Major*, revised a story, "Leaf by Niggle," worked on a new translation of *Sir Gawain and the Green Knight*, and reread *The Hobbit* and *The Silmarillion*, finding sections in *them* that he wanted to revise!

By 1967, *The Lord of the Rings* had been translated into nine languages. A year later, it had a total readership of fifty million people. In the United States, a fan club, the Tolkien Society of America, was born. In North Borneo, the Frodo Society formed — and in Vietnam, a festival dancer painted Sauron's lidless eye on his shield. Ronald received a deluge of mail. Readers thanked him, scolded him, posed questions, asked for money. Celebrities invited him to parties. President Lyndon Johnson's daughter Lynda Bird sought his autograph, and a New Yorker demanded, "Admit Middle-earth to the UN!" Amazed and rattled by the uproar, Ronald always tried to answer the letters that children wrote to him. He lost drafts of replies in his house, finding them again in piles of unfinished projects and staying awake half the night to rework them.

At age sixty-seven, he'd reached mandatory retirement at Oxford University. He was made a Professor Emeritus and presented a valedictory address before a large audience in Merton College Hall. "You have given the University four decades," he was told. "Your contributions to philology are a great beam of light."

Both retirement and fame unsettled Ronald. He had always tried to shelter himself from modern-day life, cloistered behind academia, but it was becoming more difficult. He still "traveled" on his starship to Middle-earth, still welcomed news that "came to him" of Bilbo or Frodo, but he'd lost his daily routine of lectures and meetings. C. S. Lewis died in 1963, a shattering blow.

And though Allen & Unwin provided a secretary to help answer his mail (which arrived three times a day, six days a week) and to open gifts from strangers who'd read his books, Ronald fretted over his time. If he allowed any interviews, he set an alarm clock for ten minutes after a visitor arrived, claiming when it rang that he must go to another appointment.

Popularity finally became too intrusive — fans trampled his garden to peer into windows of his house, telephoned him in the middle of the night, mobbed him in church — and he and Edith decided to move. He was grateful that *The Lord of the Rings* was a success, but he wished readers would be satisfied just to *read*. Age was taking its toll, and Edith's ill health deeply worried him. Together, they made plans to live in Bournemouth, a nearby seaside resort. Care was taken by family and friends to keep their address secret. Bournemouth residents didn't suspect that their new neighbors were named Tolkien — or that the 1966 recipient of England's famous Benson Medal, awarded for *The Lord of the Rings* by the Royal Society of Literature, was the gray-haired man with the pipe — *wasn't his name Ronald?* — who lived in the bungalow down the road.

Life in Bournemouth was peaceful. Ronald knew that the whirlwind response to his book continued, but he was no longer caught up in it. The BBC had made a documentary film about him, he'd sold movie rights for an animated version of *The Lord of the Rings* to America's United Artists studio, and he'd turned down offers from soap companies who wanted to make replicas of Frodo, Gandalf, and Sam. Most details about his book were brought to him by Joy Hill, his secretary from Allen & Unwin, but when she'd go back to London, Ronald could walk among the trees, relieved not to think about publicity.

His children, all flourishing, visited Bournemouth. Both Christopher and Michael had children and grandchildren of their own — and Ronald was a doting grandfather and great-grandfather. He'd been walking with a cane since taking a fall — but the cane was put aside when the grandchildren stopped by. He spun old tales about the villain Bill Stickers, whose name he'd taken years ago from an Oxford sign that read: BILL STICKERS WILL BE PROSECUTED. He taught his great-grandchildren to climb trees. All children, he said, have "a human intelligence which even at its lowest is a pretty wonderful thing." Called "Grandfellow" by his great-grandchildren, Ronald used portions of his royalties from Allen & Unwin to help finance their education.

In 1966, Ronald and Edith celebrated their fiftieth wedding anniversary. Friends, colleagues, and family threw a large party in Oxford's Merton Senior Common

Room, and Donald Swann, a successful composer of musical reviews, presented the anniversary couple with a collection of Ronald's poems set to music. For the first time in years, Edith sat down at a piano. No arthritis pains in her fingers could stop her from playing the songs.

Part of Ronald's desire for seclusion in Bournemouth came from his fears about Edith's health. If he was invited to have dinner in Oxford with a colleague, he wouldn't go unless Joy Hill or perhaps Hilary, visiting from his farm, stayed at Edith's side. He often cut short a stroll instead of leaving her alone. An old sadness settled in him; loss, he knew, hovered nearby. He had reached his late seventies; Edith was eighty years old. Neither of them could share the immortality of his elves. What Ronald felt for his wife was, for him, like the love of *The Silmarillion's* Beren and Lúthien. Even at eighty, Edith reminded him of Lúthien, who had danced in the woods.

On November 29, 1971, in her eighty-second year, Edith Tolkien fell ill in the night and died from an inflamed gallbladder. To the end, she'd kept reminding Ronald to use his cane so he wouldn't fall. "I'll take care of myself," he'd promised. Grief-stricken at her death, he accompanied her body by car to Wolvercote Cemetery in Oxford. At her grave, his children and Hilary surrounding him, his face was haggard, his shoulders stooped. He'd arranged for a Catholic burial, just as Father Francis had once made arrangements for Mabel Tolkien.

Ronald would later write that in their last years together, he and Edith still met "in a woodland glade," going "hand in hand many times to escape the shadow of imminent death before our last parting." In 1972, when a friend advised him to remove his wedding ring in order to lessen his grief, he flatly refused. "I am still married," Ronald said. On Middle-earth, he told his friend, Sauron's One Ring had been filled with negative power, exhausting the strength of Frodo, Gollum, or anyone wearing it—but the gold band on his own finger, worn for fifty-five years, contained the eternal powers of goodness and love.

Chapter 11

One Saturday morning, a fifteen-year-old New Yorker named Richard Plotz spied Elvish words scrawled on a subway poster. An avid fan of *The Lord of the Rings*, Plotz was shocked to see Elvish in underground New York. The next week, he found crayoned on another poster: BILBO BAGGINS IS PROBABLY A FAKE. Sayings and quips resulting from "Tolkien mania" continued to appear in the subway, and Plotz impulsively wrote a line himself: TOLKIEN CLUB MEETS AT ALMA MATER STATUE, 2:00, FEBRUARY FIFTH.

A week later, six students — none of whom had scribbled the graffiti or previously met — stood with Richard Plotz by the snowy statue at Columbia University. Happy to find each other, the little group quickly grew after Plotz put an ad in *New Republic* magazine. "DISCUSS HOBBIT LORE & LEARN ELVISH," he wrote, listing his address and signing himself "Frodo." Before long, chapters had formed across the United States, collectively calling themselves the Tolkien Society of America. Artists, lawyers, homemakers, teachers, doctors, and students discussed mythology in *The Hobbit* and *The Lord of the Rings*, wrote poetry in Elvish, drew pictures of the Shire, and ate "hobbit food" at Hobbit Picnics. W. H. Auden agreed to speak at the New York chapter, and Plotz somehow persuaded Ronald to become a member. Plotz's enthusiasm even helped prompt the birth of the Tolkien Society in Great Britain.

Though Ronald grieved over Edith, Middle-earth and its inhabitants remained constant. Ronald had claimed that his books were not invention, but discovery. Now he could say that no matter what happened to him, his mythology would survive; the Tolkien Society of America convinced him of that.

Out of respect for their famous philologist and author, Merton College offered Ronald two rooms over a garden. Unable to bear living in Bournemouth without Edith, he gratefully let movers pack up his belongings. On March 22, 1972, he left Bournemouth and settled into 21 Merton Lane, saying he would "pick up the threads" of his life. Merton elected him Honorary Fellow, a highly respected title, and once again he wore black robes in the dining hall and was invited to faculty teas. When loneliness overwhelmed him, he tried to stay busy. He went for walks or visited the trees in the Botanical Gardens. A Merton caretaker and his wife, Charles and Mavis Carr, checked on him every day, and he often chatted with Mavis in her native Welsh.

Joy Hill kept appearing from London to open the mail, cheering him as much as she could. A twinkle reappeared in his eyes if he recounted his stories of the Black and White Ogres of Sarehole or of lowering the rope outside Mrs. Faulkner's so Edith could send up pilfered food. One day, he and Joy took an especially long walk. "Professor Tolkien!" she finally gasped. "Why aren't you tired? I can hardly catch my breath."

"It's all my miles on Middle-earth," he replied, smiling. "Let's go to the Gardens. I want to show you my favorite tree, the Great Black Pine."

Talk had died down at the University about "Tolkien fairy tales" being a demeaning hobby. In June 1972, Ronald was awarded an honorary doctorate by Oxford University, presented at the Sheldonian Theatre before colleagues, friends, and family. The University's Public Orator said that Professor J.R.R. Tolkien had "alone created a new mythology such as took the Greek people centuries to elaborate." He had "come back from retirement," said the Orator, "whereby he eluded his intrusive fans. We are happy to salute him in his eightieth year."

Honors for Ronald continued to mount. Lord Snowdon, husband of England's Princess Margaret, photographed him for a Tolkien calendar. In 1973, with *The Lord of the Rings* published in France, he won the French Prize for best foreign novel of the year. His most cherished award — for his achievements in philology — was the Commander, Order of the British Empire (C.B.E.) medal, one rank below knighthood. Bestowed on him by Queen Elizabeth at Buckingham Palace, the medal was stolen from his rooms on the night he received it. Luckily, the guilt-ridden thief, who was never found, later returned it.

Some nights, Ronald still revised *The Silmarillion.* His hopes of having the book published had dimmed; so many drafts existed that he could lose weeks choosing between the different versions of one event. He no longer expected to finish the manuscript. As he wrote to Stanley Unwin, he'd made his son Christopher the heir of the project. Once or twice a month, he took the train to Allen & Unwin's offices, aghast at the burgeoning size of Oxford and London. His publishers treated him like "minor royalty," he told Joy Hill. They informed him that single orders for *The Lord of the Rings* once numbered fifty to one hundred copies; now, an order had arrived for six thousand books.

Without Edith being near to hear such news, Ronald felt extremely lonely. On the headstone he'd ordered for her grave, he had the name Lúthien carved beneath her own. Since her death, his happiest times were with his family. He visited Hilary in Evesham, took a trip with Priscilla and her son Simon, and flew kites with his two youngest grandchildren, Adam and Rachel, from Christopher's second marriage. With his steadily increasing royalties, he bought a house for one of his children, and a car for another. "I never dreamed," he said, "that I could stop struggling for money."

By the summer of 1973, Ronald was depending more on his cane. His old stomach ulcer had flared up, and his doctor put him on a strict diet. In August, he lunched carefully with Priscilla at an Oxford hotel, delighted by the gifts she'd brought him from a holiday in Austria. The next week, feeling stronger, he wrote her a note, signing it "My dearest love to you — Daddy."

On August 28, Ronald embarked on a week's visit to friends in Bournemouth. Charles Carr, the caretaker, ushered him into a taxi on Merton Street, remembering later that he'd seemed energetic. Two days later, however, Ronald collapsed with stomach pains during a party. His friends rushed him to a hospital and telephoned Priscilla. Distraught, she arranged to come at once with John. Michael and Christopher were away, one in France, the other in Switzerland.

Ronald's ulcer worsened and he developed pneumonia. Though he'd once confided to Charles Carr that he thought he might live much longer, he seemed calm and at peace as doctors examined him. Perhaps he felt that if the end were really near, he need not be afraid. He may have looked forward to a reunion with Edith, or thought of Frodo, who'd said, "It must often be so ... when things are in danger; someone has to give them up, lose them, so that others may keep them."

On the first day of September, Ronald's ulcer bled heavily and his breathing was labored. With Priscilla and John at his side, he lay with peaceful acceptance. Outside his hospital window, a few trees began shedding their leaves for autumn. Others, as beguiling as the camelthorn tree he'd once longed to climb in Bloemfontein's desert, leaned toward him with eager arms. The next morning, September 2, while Bournemouth awakened sleepily beside the sea and journalists around the world phoned Ronald's hospital room for medical reports, bells tolled on the plains and in the valleys of Middle-earth. At the age of eighty-one, leaving behind a Secondary

World so rich and splendid, so full of language and love and terror and beauty that its enchantment would hold forever, John Ronald Reuel Tolkien died.

When Ronald's name was added to the tombstone at Edith's and his gravesite in Wolvercote, the name Beren appeared under his own to match Edith's Lúthien. Four days after his death, with newspaper obituaries having appeared in many countries, a requiem Mass was held for him in Oxford, presided over in part by his son John. In November, a memorial service took place in Merton Chapel and, at another service far away in California, a reading was given from his short story "Leaf by Niggle." "Before him," a line from the story was quoted, "stood the Tree, his Tree, finished."

The bulk of Ronald's estate was left in trust for his family, with certain funds earmarked for the Birmingham Oratory, in memory of Father Francis, and for Exeter and Pembroke colleges. He'd made generous donations to several organizations for the elderly, having visited them on empty days after Edith's death. Also left in "trust" was the huge task of completing *The Silmarillion* — which, as his father's literary heir, Christopher Tolkien began.

Some chapters of the book, written nearly sixty years earlier when Ronald was a second lieutenant in World War I, were in fragments; style and tone differed from later chapters. Details had to be checked for consistency; transitions had to be added between sections. The entire manuscript needed overall editing and, sometimes, rewriting. Wanting more time to work on *The Silmarillion*, Christopher resigned from his university post and moved with his family to France. There, he labored for several years on the manuscript.

In September 1977, fulfilling Ronald's persistent wish, *The Silmarillion* was simultaneously published by Allen & Unwin and Houghton Mifflin. Both publishers expected loyal fans to buy the book, but they found the text more stilted than *The Lord of the Rings* and predicted only average sales. What followed was a publishing milestone. Advance orders for *The Silmarillion* were so huge that the book sold out on its way to stores. Printers couldn't keep up with the avalanche of orders, especially since replicas of a map drawn by Christopher had to be pasted by hand into each copy. *The Silmarillion* began selling to frustrated store owners at black-market prices. Houghton Mifflin meted out copies as if they were rationed food, allowing each store only a portion of any order. By December 1977, one million copies of the book were in print.

Reviews of *The Silmarillion*, with a few exceptions, did not reflect the public's fervor. "Empty and pompous," said the *New York Review of Books*. "Unreadable," said

London's *Times Literary Supplement*. Yet Ronald's more than half-century effort had not been undertaken for commercial sale. His book was classical in style, written in the formal language of Old Norse or Anglo-Saxon legends. What he'd created was an ingenious and poetic mythology of the world's beginnings to its Age of Man. *The Silmarillion* was a grand tapestry on which hung the tales of *The Hobbit* and *The Lord of the Rings*. Its success may have come from its readers, particularly young people, sensing that Ronald Tolkien was not a cynic or phony—but, like the Silmarils themselves, genuine and true.

Soon, Christopher had released more of his father's unknown work. In the 1980s Allen & Unwin and Houghton Mifflin published *Unfinished Tales of Numenor and Middle-earth*; *The Book of Lost Tales, Part I and Part II*; *The Lays of Beleriand*; and *The Shaping of Middle-earth*, among others. By then, an American Tolkien Society, organized in 1972, had issued a quarterly journal and sponsored Tolkien Week and Hobbit Day. In Maine, the New England Tolkien Society listed Ronald's academic publications, and, in Milwaukee, Wisconsin, Marquette University had purchased the original manuscripts of *The Hobbit* and *The Lord of the Rings*.

Ronald's fantasy stories and novels are still a publishing industry today. *The Lord of the Rings* has been translated into more than thirty-five languages, and both the trilogy and *The Hobbit* have sold many millions of copies. Tolkien dictionaries appear in libraries — along with a host of books analyzing Middle-earth's mythology, languages, and various species. Christopher Tolkien, representing the Tolkien estate, has continued to release his father's work, including *The Legend of Sigurd and Gudrún; The Children of Húrin;* and *Roverandom.*

A new generation is discovering Middle-earth. Many readers will never know that the creator of Frodo Baggins, Ring-bearer on a journey of terrible fear and heart-wrenching glory, was a professor of philology who could lecture in Gothic and changed our knowledge of language. Such readers, however, may share a common response, finding in Middle-earth a deep coming-home, as if a part of themselves has gone into reading J.R.R. Tolkien — and Middle-earth belongs to them.

Ronald's work, said Paul Ritz, an officer of the American Tolkien Society, has "something for everyone. He didn't just write a book. He wrote a world." In that world of song and sunlight is also fierce danger. Yet Ronald Tolkien wanted us to know that even while the fires of Mordor burn darkly, even when tomorrow may seem unsure, we can use our imaginations, courage, and strength to seek the splendor in life.

On his odyssey with Frodo, Sam once looked up

from the desolation on the ground to see a white star twinkling in the night. Awed by its radiance amid Mordor's evil, he suddenly understood that "in the end the Shadow was only a small and passing thing: there was light and high beauty for ever beyond its reach."

Perhaps, then, Ronald's dragons may finally quiet their fire and rest their heads beneath the sheltering trees.

Writings by J.R.R. Tolkien

1915   Poem: "Goblin Feet." In *Oxford Poetry*, 1915. Edited by G. D. H. Cole and T. W. Earp. Oxford: B. H. Blackwell, 64–65.

1922   *A Middle English Vocabulary*. Oxford: Clarendon Press.

1925   *Sir Gawain and the Green Knight*. Edited by J.R.R. Tolkien and E. V. Gordon. Oxford: Clarendon Press. (Issued in paperback, 1968.)

   "Some Contributions to Middle-English Lexicography." *Review of English Studies* 1, no. 2 (April 1925): 210–15.

1929   "*Ancrene Wisse* and *Hali Meiðhad*." *Essays and Studies* 14: 104–26.

1934 "Chaucer as a Philologist: *The Reeve's Tale.*" In *Transactions of the Philological Society.* London: David Nutt, 1–70.

1936 *Songs for the Philologists.* J.R.R. Tolkien, E. V. Gordon, et al. Privately printed by the Department of English, University College, London. (A collection of humorous verses, originally distributed at Leeds University.)

1937 *The Hobbit, or There and Back Again.* London: George Allen & Unwin Ltd. (First U.S. edition — Boston: Houghton Mifflin Company, 1938.)

"*Beowulf:* The Monsters and the Critics." *Proceedings of the British Academy* 22 (1936): 245–95. London: Oxford University Press. (Reprinted in U.S. by Notre Dame Press [1963] and Prentice-Hall [1968].)

1945 "Leaf by Niggle." *Dublin Review* 432 (January 1945): 46–61. London: Burns, Oates, & Washbourne Ltd.

1947 "On Fairy-Stories." In *Essays Presented to Charles Williams.* Edited by C. S. Lewis. London: Oxford University Press, 38–89.

1949   *Farmer Giles of Ham.* London: George Allen & Unwin Ltd.

1953   "The Homecoming of Beorhtnoth Beorhthelm's Son." *Essays and Studies by Members of the English Association,* New Series, Vol. VI. London: John Murray, 1–18.

1954   *The Fellowship of the Ring: Being the First Part of The Lord of the Rings.* London: George Allen & Unwin Ltd. (First U.S. edition — Boston: Houghton Mifflin Company, 1954.)

      The Two Towers: Being the Second Part of The Lord of the Rings. London: George Allen & Unwin Ltd. (First U.S. edition — Boston: Houghton Mifflin Company, 1955.)

1955   *The Return of the King: Being the Third Part of The Lord of the Rings.* London: George Allen & Unwin Ltd. (First U.S. edition   Boston: Houghton Mifflin Company, 1955. *The Lord of the Rings* edition, New York: Ace Books, 1965; New York: Ballantine Books, 1965.)

1962   *Ancrene Wisse: The English Text of the Ancrene Riwle.*

Edited by J.R.R. Tolkien. Vol. 249, Early English Text Society. London: Oxford University Press.

The Adventures of Tom Bombadil and Other Verses from the Red Book. London: George Allen & Unwin Ltd.

1964　*Tree and Leaf.* London: George Allen & Unwin Ltd. (A reprint of "On Fairy-Stories" and "Leaf by Niggle." First U.S. edition—Boston: Houghton Mifflin Company, 1965.)

1965　Poems: "Once Upon a Time" and "The Dragon's Visit." In *Winter's Tales for Children 1.* Edited by Caroline Hillier. London: Macmillan, 45–45 and 84–87. (Published simultaneously in U.S.—New York: St. Martin's Press. Reprinted in *The Young Magicians.* Edited by Lin Carter. New York: Ballantine Books, 1969, 254–62.)

1966　*The Tolkien Reader.* New York: Ballantine Books. (A reprint of "The Homecoming of Beorhtnoth," "On Fairy-Stories," "Leaf by Niggle," *Farmer Giles of Ham,* and *The Adventures of Tom Bombadil.*)

1967 *Smith of Wootton Major.* London: George Allen & Unwin Ltd.

1968 *The Road Goes Ever On: A Song-Cycle,* with music by Donald Swann. London: George Allen & Unwin Ltd.

1973 Poem: "The Hoard." In *The Hamish Hamilton Book of Dragons.* Edited by Roger Lancelyn Green. London: Hamish Hamilton, 246–48.

1975 *Sir Gawain and the Green Knight, Pearl,* and *Sir Orfeo.* Translated by J.R.R. Tolkien. Edited and with a preface by Christopher Tolkien. London: George Allen & Unwin Ltd.

1976 *The Father Christmas Letters.* Edited by Baillie Tolkien. London: George Allen & Unwin Ltd. Boston: Houghton Mifflin Company. (New edition, paperback — Boston: Houghton Mifflin Company, 1991.)

1977 *The Silmarillion.* Edited by Christopher Tolkien. London: George Allen & Unwin Ltd. (First U.S. edition — Boston: Houghton Mifflin Company, 1977.)

1980 *Unfinished Tales.* Edited by Christopher Tolkien. London: George Allen & Unwin Ltd. Boston: Houghton Mifflin Company.

1981 *The Letters of J.R.R. Tolkien.* Selected and edited by Humphrey Carpenter with the assistance of Christopher Tolkien. Boston: Houghton Mifflin Company.

1982 *Mr. Bliss.* London: George Allen & Unwin Ltd. Boston: Houghton Mifflin Company, 1983.

Finn and Hengest: The Fragment and the Episode. Edited by Alan Bliss. London: George Allen & Unwin Ltd. Boston: Houghton Mifflin Company, 1983.

The Old English Exodus. Edited by Joan Turville-Petre. England: Oxford University Press.

1983 *The Book of Lost Tales, Part 1: The History of Middle-earth.* Edited by Christopher Tolkien. London: George Allen & Unwin Ltd. Boston: Houghton Mifflin Company, 1984.

1984 *The Book of Lost Tales, Part II: The History of Middle-earth.* Edited by Christopher Tolkien. London:

George Allen & Unwin Ltd. Boston: Houghton Mifflin Company.

1985 *The Lays of Beleriand.* Edited by Christopher Tolkien. London: George Allen & Unwin Ltd. Boston: Houghton Mifflin Company.

1986 *The Shaping of Middle-earth: The Quenta, the Ambarkanta, and the Annals.* Edited by Christopher Tolkien. London: George Allen & Unwin Ltd. Boston: Houghton Mifflin Company.

1987 *The Lost Road and Other Writings.* Edited by Christopher Tolkien. London: Unwin Hyman Ltd. Boston: Houghton Mifflin Company.

1988 *The Return of the Shadow.* London: Unwin Hyman Ltd. Boston: Houghton Mifflin Company.

1989 Poetry: *Oliphant.* Chicago: Contemporary Books.

The Treason of Isengard. Edited by Christopher Tolkien. London: Unwin Hyman Ltd. Boston: Houghton Mifflin Company.

1990 *The War of the Ring.* Edited by Christopher Tolkien.

London: Unwin Hyman Ltd. Boston: Houghton Mifflin Company.

1992 *Sauron Defeated*. Edited by Christopher Tolkien. London: HarperCollins Publishers. Boston: Houghton Mifflin Company.

1993 *Morgoth's Ring*. London: HarperCollins Publishers. Boston: Houghton Mifflin Company.

1994 *The War of the Jewels*. Edited by Christopher Tolkien. London: HarperCollins Publishers. Boston: Houghton Mifflin Company.

1998 *Roverandom*. Edited by Christina Scull and Wayne G. Hammond. London: HarperCollins Publishers. Boston: Houghton Mifflin Company.

2007 *The Children of Húrin*. Edited by Christopher Tolkien. London: HarperCollins Publishers. Boston: Houghton Mifflin Company.

2009 *The Legend of Sigurd and Gudrún*. Edited by Christopher Tolkien. London: HarperCollins Publishers. Boston: Houghton Mifflin Harcourt.

Index

31901051751057